ENGLISH MANOR HOUSES

ENGLISH MANOR HOUSES

TEXT BY

Nicholas Cooper

PHOTOGRAPHS BY

Marianne Majerus

WEIDENFELD & NICOLSON
LONDON

First published in Great Britain in 1990 by George Weidenfeld & Nicolson Limited,
91 Clapham High Street, London SW4 7TA

British Library Cataloguing in Publication Data
Cooper, Nicholas
English manor houses.
1. England. Manor houses, history
I. Title
942

ISBN 0 297 83045 7

Typeset by Keyspools Ltd, Golborne, Lancs, UK
Colour separations by Newsele Litho
Printed by Printers SRL, Trento, Italy
Bound by L.E.G.O. Vicenza, Italy

Endpapers: Beckley Park, Oxfordshire (see also pp. 68, 146).
p.1: East Barsham Manor, Norfolk (see also pp. 27, 110, 111, 118, 147).
p.2: Broughton Castle, Oxfordshire. More a fortified manor house than a true castle, it was already a grand and complex house when it was bought by William of Wykeham in 1377 (see also pp. 67, 97, 103).

CONTENTS

NOTE ABOUT THE PROPERTIES

It should be noted that many of the houses featured in this book are strictly private. A few like Gravetye Manor and Nappa Hall operate as hotels or bed-and-breakfasts. According to information published in early 1990, those that can be visited are listed below, together with available telephone numbers. (More information about locations may be given here than in the captions, which only list towns or villages when they are not part of the name of the house itself.) Fuller details about opening times, admission charges, etc. can normally be found in relevant guidebooks like *Historic Houses, Castles and Gardens* or ascertained from the house itself.

HOUSES OPEN

National Trust

Bradley Manor, Newton Abbot, Devon
Buckland Abbey, Yelverton, Devon (0822 853607)
Great Chalfield Manor, nr Melksham, Wiltshire
Ightham Mote, Ivy Hatch, Kent (Plaxtol 810378)
Lower Brockhampton, Bromyard, Hereford and Worcester
Newark Park, Ozleworth, Wotton-under-Edge, Gloucestershire (Dursley 842644)
Rufford Old Hall, Rufford, nr Ormskirk, Lancashire (0704 821254)

English Heritage

Old Soar, Plaxtol, Kent
Stokesay Castle, Craven Arms, Shropshire (0588 672544)

Others

Broughton Castle, Banbury, Oxfordshire (0295 262624)
Hall I' Th' Wood, Bolton, Greater Manchester (0204 51159)
Markenfield Hall, nr Ripon, North Yorkshire
Poundisford Park, Pitminster, nr Taunton, Somerset (082342 244)
Sandford Orcas, Sherbone, Dorset (096322 206)

HOUSES OPEN BY APPOINTMENT ONLY

Ashleworth Court, Ashleworth, nr Gloucester, Gloucestershire (Hartpury 241)
Elsdon Tower, Elsdon, Northumberland (Otterburn 20688)
Newhouse Farm, Goodrich, Ross-on-Wye, Hereford and Worcester
The Old (Norman) Manor House, Boothy Pagnell, Lincolnshire
Preston Patrick Hall, Milnthorpe, Cumbria (Crooklands 200)
Woodsford Castle, Woodsford, Dorset (Contact: The Landmark Trust, Shottesbrooke, nr Maidenhead, Berks)

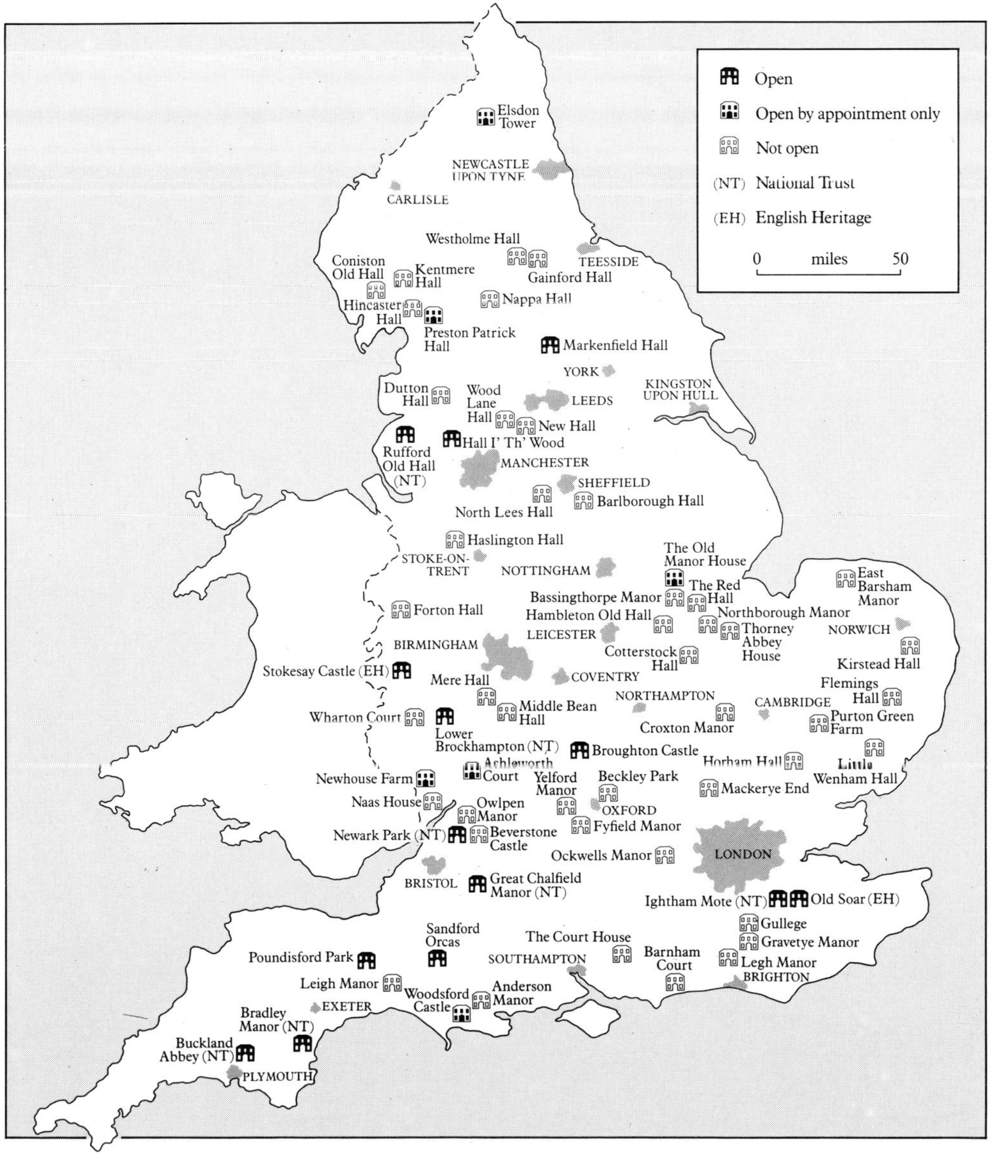
Open
Open by appointment only
Not open
(NT) National Trust
(EH) English Heritage
0 miles 50
Elsdon Tower
NEWCASTLE UPON TYNE
CARLISLE
Westholme Hall
TEESSIDE
Gainford Hall
Coniston Old Hall
Kentmere Hall
Nappa Hall
Hincaster Hall
Preston Patrick Hall
Markenfield Hall
YORK
KINGSTON UPON HULL
Dutton Hall
Wood Lane Hall
LEEDS
New Hall
Hall I' Th' Wood
Rufford Old Hall (NT)
MANCHESTER
SHEFFIELD
Barlborough Hall
North Lees Hall
Haslington Hall
STOKE-ON-TRENT
NOTTINGHAM
The Old Manor House
The Red Hall
East Barsham Manor
Bassingthorpe Manor
Hambleton Old Hall
Northborough Manor
Forton Hall
LEICESTER
Thorney Abbey House
NORWICH
BIRMINGHAM
Cotterstock Hall
Kirstead Hall
Stokesay Castle (EH)
Mere Hall
COVENTRY
Flemings Hall
NORTHAMPTON
CAMBRIDGE
Middle Bean Hall
Purton Green Farm
Wharton Court
Croxton Manor
Lower Brockhampton (NT)
Broughton Castle
Horham Hall
Little Wenham Hall
Achleworth Court
Newhouse Farm
Yelford Manor
Beckley Park
Mackerye End
Naas House
Owlpen Manor
OXFORD
Fyfield Manor
Newark Park (NT)
Beverstone Castle
Ockwells Manor
LONDON
BRISTOL
Great Chalfield Manor (NT)
Ightham Mote (NT)
Old Soar (EH)
Gullege
Gravetye Manor
Sandford Orcas
The Court House
Poundisford Park
SOUTHAMPTON
Barnham Court
Legh Manor
BRIGHTON
Leigh Manor
Anderson Manor
Woodsford Castle
EXETER
Bradley Manor (NT)
Buckland Abbey (NT)
PLYMOUTH

I

THE MANOR AND ITS PEOPLE

CROXTON MANOR
Cambridgeshire

Croxton Manor shows how misleading names can be. There were already two manors in the village of Croxton when they were recorded in Domesday Book in 1087, and by the end of the thirteenth century there were four. The house illustrated here seems actually to have belonged to a manor called Westbury, and though built in the late Middle Ages it is neither the original house of that manor nor even on the site of it. There is nothing unusual about this sort of confusion: in fact, it is much less common to know who a house belonged to, or even whether or not it actually was the manor house, than to find a place like Croxton where the situation was complicated to begin with and where lost records and false traditions have made unravelling it even harder.

Most people cherish an ideal picture of the manor house as a house that is large, old but comfortable, dignified without being grand, and the home of an ancient family that has been there time out of mind. But this picture is only partly true. Many villages had no manor houses, and some had more than one. Lords of the manor might devote the best part of their lives to the local community where they lived, or they might be absentees, owning a dozen manors and caring little or nothing about any of them. And over the length and breadth of England and through five hundred years of history, varying local conditions and constant change have meant that manor houses differ widely in size, in layout and in grandeur.

Furthermore, although all the houses in this book look like manor houses of one sort or another, not all of them are. Names can be misleading – people have surprisingly often changed the name of their house, say from Manor to Lodge, to House, even to Castle (if in the right style of architecture) and back again. Some manor houses came down in the world and became (and were called) farms; the same has happened in reverse, too, so some houses are called Manors that never were. In some parts of the country manor houses were anyway known by other names, such as Courts or Halls. Without knowing the detailed history of the building it is not always possible to know whether it was ever the actual home of the man who was lord of the manor. The size is not much guide, either: there were poor, small manors as well as large ones with great houses for their lords.

There is another reason why not all the houses included here are strictly manor houses. Although in the Middle Ages few people built a dignified house unless they were lords of the manor or even grander, later on there were increasing numbers of people who aspired to the class of the gentry yet never acquired a manor, though they built houses fit for a lord of the manor to live in. Other houses in this book, like hunting lodges, for example, were built for living in on particular occasions, by people who may have had manors and manor houses elsewhere. So this book is about houses that could have been manor houses as well as about those that actually were, and about how the idea of the manor house came to be accepted as an ideal by the ever-increasing numbers of the gentry.

In the Middle Ages the occupants of most manor houses were knights or esquires rather than the greatest men of the land. Members of the nobility were lords of manors as well, but they lived very different lives, involved as they often were with the highest affairs of state and having vast incomes to match their high titles. Consequently the castles and great houses that were their principal homes were different in character and function, as well as in size, from the majority of homes of those lesser members of the upper classes. Some manor houses were built for the occasional visits of these great men or for their officials, but most of those illustrated here were for living in all the year round rather than for staying in (sometimes with a huge train of retainers) during a great man's brief visit to one part of his vast domain.

There were manors, as distinct from manor houses, all over England. Manors were established before the Norman Conquest, when Saxon kings gave estates and authority to their chief men in return for their help and support in times of war. William the Conqueror kept up the system and strengthened it, giving great domains to his principal followers who in turn often granted individual manors to followers of theirs. The manor was a mixture of private estate and administrative area, where the lord of the manor both owned the land which his tenants farmed, and meted out justice to everyone who lived there. It sounds a tyrannical arrangement, and sometimes it was. Most villagers were the lord's tenants, and they had to pay him rent or work on his land, and (if they farmed themselves, and in the Middle Ages a high proportion of villagers did) they were obliged to lend their oxen to plough the lord's own farm (his 'demesne') and their horses and carts to carry his crops. They owed him other services as well. For example, they might have to grind their corn at the lord's mill (at his prices), could not marry or leave home without his permission (for which they had to pay), and the son of a tenant often had to give the lord one of his best beasts before he could inherit his father's tenancy. There could be no question about the lord of the manor being the most important person in the place.

What generally saved the system from being grossly exploitative was that it was based largely upon rules and traditions of the villagers' own devising and laws concerned with their own welfare. There were rules about how the fields of the village should be farmed, rules about straying beasts, rules about cleaning ditches and

NEW HALL
Elland, West Yorkshire

New Hall was built in the 1490s by Nicholas Savile, a member of a gentry family with extensive property in the area, and it remained in the hands of the Saviles until 1620. By 1650 the house was the property of Henry Power, a distinguished physician and polymath, who became one of the first Fellows of the Royal Society and whose writings and experiments embraced (besides anatomy and medicine) such diverse subjects as sun-spots, magnetism, the Hebrew alphabet, botany, microscopy, and discoveries in coal mines. It was almost certainly Power who added the stone front to the house. Wide-ranging as his interests were, it is unlikely that they extended to architecture: the style of his house is typical of the district and shows no awareness of building developments elsewhere.
See also pp. 125, 148.

mending roads, rules that prohibited men from encroaching on their neighbours' lands, and rules for appointing the village officials who had to enforce them. There were traditions (called 'the customs of the manor' and differing from one place to another) about who had the right to inherit land and how and where beasts could pasture. These had been formulated by the village farmers themselves or inherited from their forefathers. Though men often questioned whether the lord's exactions might not be more than he was entitled to, almost nobody ever questioned the basis of the system.

As lord of the manor, and (often) as a justice of the peace as well, the lord administered laws concerned with keeping the peace and punishing petty criminals. He (or his agent, the reeve) enforced the customs of the manor in the manor court, which gave weight to his authority while he exercised it partly for the villagers' own benefit. Thus the lord of the manor was as important in the community as the source of justice and authority as he was as owner of the village land.

Not that the system was ever as uniform as this suggests. There were manors everywhere, but some were small, some were large; some manors were the only ones that their lords possessed, while others were the property of great landowners who might have dozens. The noblemen who were the lords of many manors might own great houses or even castles in some, and in others no more than a simple building where the manor court could be held and where perhaps a steward might live. Bishoprics and abbeys owned manors, too, which had often been given as a source of income and which were administered by their staff. Some of these manors also had fine houses, where the bishop himself, the abbot or prior might stay on occasion. More often, the manor house on a church estate was much like that on the lesser estates of great noblemen. The system was further complicated by the fact that manors were property and could be inherited, sold, split up between heirs and heiresses and consolidated again. Sometimes a manor comprised the whole of a village; elsewhere, a village might come to be divided between several manors, with those who lived in different parts of the village serving different lords. Noblemen who owned many manors might sell them when they were hard up, and new men on the way up could make their mark by buying them. With the dissolution of the monasteries by Henry VIII a huge number of manors that had belonged to the church were confiscated by the king, only to be sold off piecemeal or given to laymen.

As we have seen, the manor house was intimately connected with the life of the community, since it was here that so many decisions were taken that affected the villagers' lives. Sometimes the location of the manor house still shows this, standing close to the village centre and the church (which had often been built by one of the village's early lords). But the manor house is now often situated some way from the village centre. This is sometimes because a former lord of the manor wanted to distance himself from the village, and sometimes because the village itself has moved away. This has often happened in the quite recent past. Particularly in the eighteenth century, it was not uncommon for landowners to pull down whole villages and rebuild them at a distance in order to make space for a park adjoining the great house. In earlier centuries, however, villages sometimes moved for reasons that are not so well understood. In the Middle Ages villagers' houses were often poor and ill built and might not last more than a generation or two. They might then be replaced by a new house in a better position – nearer to a spring, perhaps, or to neighbours – and so by degrees a village might move, leaving the more substantial buildings, the church and the manor house, behind. In other cases the village has largely or even completely disappeared, possibly during the great fall in population that occurred during the fourteenth and fifteenth centuries during and after the Black Death, when within 150 years the number of people in England fell by as much as a half.

For any of these reasons the manor house might be left standing out on its own, far from the nearest buildings of the village, and the number of pictures in this book showing the manor house remote from other houses demonstrates how often this occurred. Such changes also illustrate the extent to which the function of the manor house has altered over the centuries, as its lord became gradually more remote from the life of the village community. Changes began early. Once, lords of manors had to pay the king with the service of an armed knight; if a manor was divided in two, the two new manors were liable for half a knight each, and the only way of providing that was by paying money. The king might anyway prefer to be paid money and to hire good soldiers himself. There were many reasons why lords of the manor themselves might prefer to have cash rents paid them by their tenants rather than to have them working on the demesne farm. Once the notion of personal services began to be supplanted by cash the relations between lords and villagers inevitably changed, too.

The system whereby the village community was subject to rules established and enforced at the manor court lasted in some places until the eighteenth or nineteenth centuries, but it had been changing for many generations before that. Modern tenures were taking the place of traditional ones, men were increasingly subject to the laws of the land rather than to the customs of the manor, and when the lands of the village were no longer farmed in common there ceased to be the need to make rules in common for their management.

As the manor was gradually, over the ages, taking on more the function of a modern estate, so at the same time newcomers bought land and built themselves handsome houses. Some rich men, particularly around London and a few other large towns, bought estates that were quite small but on which they might build a house worthy of their wealth and status. Increasingly, from the fifteenth and sixteenth centuries on, men who had made money in the law, at Court, in business, as the right-hand-men of great noblemen, and even as successful tenant farmers, were buying land both as a way of acquiring prestige and as a way of disposing capital that provided a safe long-term investment. For such men owning land was what mattered, whether or not it also brought with it manorial rights. And these new landowners also needed houses.

Most of the houses included here are manor houses, though some are not. Some have stayed in the same families for many generations, while others have changed hands frequently. Some are among the oldest houses that still stand in England; some are only three hundred years old. Some were built by men who had inherited ancient estates; others were built by new landowners on property they had amassed themselves. Some were always the homes of their owners; others were visited only occasionally. They were the homes of squires, merchants and clergymen, of famous families, and of owners now forgotten and unknown. But each one of them encapsulates some aspect of the history of England.

YELFORD MANOR
Oxfordshire

Yelford is typical of hundreds of small manor houses up and down the country in having no known history. It is in the upper Thames Valley in quiet, still rather remote countryside, and Yelford village has shrunk almost to nothing. The house was probably built in the late fifteenth century and modernised in the late sixteenth or early seventeenth, a period when very many houses were brought up to date as rising standards of living led owners to improve homes which they could not afford to rebuild. See also pp. 98, 141.

NAPPA HALL
Askrigg, West Yorkshire

Built around the middle of the fifteenth century, Nappa Hall is a fortified house with thick-walled battlemented towers at each end, although the hall itself is unfortified and a lower wing projecting forward on the right was added in the seventeenth century when all need for fortification was long passed. By the sixteenth century the Metcalfes of Nappa were among the leading families of Yorkshire, but they overstretched themselves, and lawsuits and buying land on mortgage led to their holding little by the mid-seventeenth century save Nappa itself. The last of the Metcalfes of Nappa died in 1756; a subsequent owner bankrupted himself with an unsuccessful local cotton mill, and by the early twentieth century the house was used by the Vyner family of Studley Royal (a far grander place) for grouse shooting parties. It is now a comfortable, working farmhouse where the farmer's wife provides bed and breakfast for visitors. See also p. 137.

THE COURT HOUSE
East Meon, Hampshire

East Meon Court House was built in the 1390s on part of the vast domain of the Bishops of Winchester. The Court House is on the right in this view, the church on the left, and the Downs rise up behind the village. It is unlikely that the bishop ever came here; he had greater palaces to visit when he toured his estates, and the Court House, as its name suggests, was simply a manor house whose principal function was to provide a hall for the meetings of the manor court and accommodation for the bishop's officials. Different lords ran their manors in different ways, and absentees were not always the best: in the middle of the fifteenth century the villagers of East Meon complained to the king himself that the bishop was trying to demand from them more money and services than he was entitled to. See also p. 54.

NORTHBOROUGH MANOR
Cambridgeshire

Northborough Manor was built in the 1330s or 1340s, possibly by Roger de Northborough, Bishop of Lichfield and briefly Lord Treasurer of England. So great a man will have had many manors, but since his name suggests that this was the village from which he came, perhaps he had a motive to lavish money on what is a sophisticated but not particularly large manor house. He may even have lived here (rather than just visiting it occasionally as one of his many estates) after his disgrace in 1340 due to his failure, as Lord Treasurer, to raise taxes urgently needed by King Edward III to pay his armies in France. See also pp. 55, 106, 107.

MARKENFIELD HALL
Nr Ripon, North Yorkshire

In the Middle Ages the Markenfield family seem to have involved themselves in most major events in northern England, and their end came when they too often found themselves on the wrong side. They were prominent among local opponents of King Richard II; they were leaders in the northern revolt against Edward IV in 1469: they fought the Scots at Flodden in 1513; they joined the Pilgrimage of Grace in 1539, the unsuccessful northern protest against the dissolution of the monasteries, and the last completed the family's ruin by involving himself in the northern rising of 1569 on behalf of Mary, Queen of Scots. When the rising failed he fled abroad, his younger brother was arrested, and the ancient Markenfield lands were forfeited to the Crown. See also p. 47.

ASHLEWORTH COURT
Gloucestershire

During the Middle Ages the manor of Ashleworth belonged to the Abbey of St Augustine in Bristol, and the house now called Ashleworth Court was the manor house of the village. It is a remarkably well preserved stone-built house of the middle of the fifteenth century. Like many ecclesiastical manor houses, however, Ashleworth Court seems to have been built as a centre for administration rather than for the personal use of the lord of the manor; the abbot had another house (which still stands and is now misleadingly called Ashleworth Manor) where he would stay when he visited the village.

KENTMERE HALL
Cumbria

According to romantic (though improbable) tradition, Kentmere was given by King John to a certain Richard Gilpin as a reward for killing a particularly ferocious wild boar. In 1517 it was the birthplace of Bernard Gilpin who, although (as a younger son) he never became lord of the manor himself, exemplified the best kind of paternalism to be found among those who did. He entered the church and became rector of Houghton-le-Spring where he founded and ran a school, provided dinner for all his parishioners every Sunday throughout the winter (seating the poor and the better-off at separate tables); he travelled throughout the county to preach the gospel and refused to be made Bishop of Durham because it would mean leaving his people. He died after being knocked down by a bull in Durham marketplace.

CONISTON OLD HALL
Cumbria

Coniston Old Hall, in the Lake District, was built in the sixteenth century by the Fleming family, and by the early twentieth century had become in part a farmhouse and in part a barn whose great doorway was cut into the hall wall. By then the lord of the manor lived elsewhere, but his steward was still holding annual manor courts there, usually in June, to grant and renew leases on payment of a customary 'entry fine' of a number of years' rent. Payment for a new lease was also exacted when a lord died. (These were ancient 'copyhold' tenures, so called because instead of a title deed the occupier had a copy of the entry in the Court Roll that recorded the grant of his tenancy. Copyhold tenures had once been common on most manors but were superseded by modern leases and then finally abolished by law in 1922.) See also p. 109.

PRESTON PATRICK HALL
Cumbria

Preston Patrick belonged to the Patrick family until the late seventeenth century. The last of the family was a Roman Catholic priest who, when his elder brother died without children, renounced his vows and married so as to try to keep the family line alive. Unfortunately he only had daughters, and when his wife died he rejoined the priesthood and the old house passed into other hands. In spite of a good deal of rebuilding, several of the original windows and doors of the medieval house are still in place – enough to show reasonably clearly what the house must have looked like. It is now, however, a working farm house, having escaped the over-restoration that might have befallen it had it been in the richer south of England.

GREAT CHALFIELD MANOR

Nr Melksham, Wiltshire

The building of Great Chalfield was made possible by its owner's determination and litigiousness, and in both he was typical of his age. Thomas Tropnell, a clothier, was distantly related to the Percy family who had come to England with William the Conqueror, and whose ownership of the manor of Chalfield came to an end in 1356 when Sir Harry Percy died on a pilgrimage to Jerusalem. Confusion followed: he left an only daughter, while his widow, consoling herself as the mistress of the Bishop of Salisbury, refused to give the place up and in due course outlived three more husbands. Tropnell fought his way into the property by endless lawsuits with other claimants, and only obtained final possession of it in 1467, having been at law for thirty years. By the time he died he had acquired six other manors, but Great Chalfield, where he built the existing house, was his principal home. See also p. 62.

FYFIELD MANOR

Oxfordshire

In the past, when large houses have become old-fashioned, they have often been rebuilt only in part: owners have been reluctant to waste money on an entirely new house if parts of the old one could still be made to serve their purpose. Fyfield Manor is a medieval house that was brought up to date at the end of the sixteenth century, when the original hall was pulled down and a new one built in its place, leaving part of the old building still standing.

Fyfield Manor was given to St John's College, Oxford, as part of its original endowment by Sir Thomas White, alderman of London. The College then leased the house back to the Whites, and a later member of the family carried out the rebuilding. Fyfield Manor now houses the Rare Books department of Basil Blackwell, the famous Oxford publisher and bookseller. See also p. 94.

RUFFORD OLD HALL
Lancashire

Rufford was the home of the Hesketh family for six hundred years. Like many old houses, it was modernised more than once, until, when ancient buildings began to be thought of as romantic rather than merely uncomfortable, it was restored to what people imagined to have been its original state. The oldest part of the house is the timber-framed great hall, built around 1500. The brick wing on the left was added in 1662, replacing an earlier range with a suite of more up-to-date rooms. In the eighteenth century the family abandoned the old house altogether and built a smart new house a few hundred yards away in the park; in 1822 they restored the old house (while continuing to live in the new one). Finally, in 1846, they moved to a still grander house in Northamptonshire, when Sir Thomas Hesketh married Lady Anne Fermor of Easton Neston. See also p. 61.

EAST BARSHAM MANOR
Norfolk

East Barsham, even in its partly ruined state, is a spectacular house. It was built during the 1520s or 1530s by Sir Henry Fermor or by his son, Sir William – landowners of great wealth, clearly, but who made no mark nationally. Some idea of the family's standard of living is given by Sir Henry's will, made in 1533. Leaving the bulk of his property to his son, he still provided for his widow, Dame Winifred, 'a lodging in the east end of the house during her widowhood, with £20 towards hanging the same and trimming the chamber, a bason and ewer of silver, a nest of gilt goblets, a dozen of silver spoons, two goblets, two salts and a plain piece [probably some kind of silver dish without ornament], with meat and drink for herself, two maids and a man.' See also pp. 1, 110, 111, 118, 147.

BASSINGTHORPE MANOR
Lincolnshire

Bassingthorpe Manor survives as a fragment of a manor house in a fragment of a village. Bassingthorpe now contains only half a dozen scattered houses, the manor house and the church, and, like the village, the manor house was once a good deal larger. The part that now stands was added to an older house in 1569 by Sir Thomas Coney. The Coneys had been at Bassingthorpe for several generations, and Sir Thomas seems to have made money as a merchant of Calais and then retired to modernise the ancestral home; subsequent owners have pulled down all but Sir Thomas's additions. Though it was quite common for younger sons of good families to make their own way in trade or the law, it seems less usual for new money to be spent on the family's old house. See also p. 116.

GRAVETYE MANOR
Nr East Grinstead, Sussex

Gravetye was built just after 1600 by Richard Infield, an ironmaster. The manor of Gravetye is first recorded only in 1571, and it is likely that the land was carved out of a larger estate when it was bought by Infield's father. Gravetye's wealth lay not so much in farming and farm rents as in industry: in the sixteenth and seventeenth centuries Sussex was the greatest producer of iron in England, and Gravetye foundry was still casting cannons for the armed forces in the 1740s. In the late nineteenth century the house was the home of William Robinson, one of those who, with Gertrude Jekyll, revolutionised Victorian gardening with a much greater informality of planting and a revived interest in herbaceous plants. Gravetye Manor is now an exceedingly comfortable hotel. See also p. 120.

BUCKLAND ABBEY
Nr Yelverton, Devon

Buckland Abbey is a bizarre mixture of Tudor house and medieval church. Originally a Cistercian abbey, it was confiscated by Henry VIII and given to the Grenvilles, who converted the church into a country house: the nave became the hall, the chancel became service rooms, and the principal stair was built into one of the transepts.

Buckland was the home, successively, of two of the greatest Elizabethan seamen. First was Sir Richard Grenville, whose distinguished career was crowned by his stupendous fight against the Spanish in the Azores in 1591, only surrendering when, out of a crew of 150, no more than 20 were left alive. The abbey was subsequently owned by Sir Francis Drake. The house is a glorious bodge, so to speak: one feels that its owners may have had more important things to think about than architecture.

BARLBOROUGH HALL
Derbyshire

Barlborough Hall was built in the 1580s for Sir Francis Rodes, a successful, self-made Derbyshire lawyer, Justice of the Common Pleas and seneschal to the Earl of Shrewsbury. As judge he was one of those who tried Mary, Queen of Scots, while as seneschal he would probably have been responsible for administering justice on the great Earl's many manors. Until the seventeenth century men of ability would often make their way in the world by attaching themselves to the households of noblemen, and Barlborough Hall shows that posts like that held by Rodes could be highly lucrative. See also p. 108.

GAINFORD HALL
Durham

Gainford is in the north, but it is similar to some of the most up-to-date houses of its time in the Home Counties. It was built in 1600 for John Cradock, who had inherited the estate from his father and elder brothers, and who subsequently acquired further property elsewhere, to which he eventually moved. He was a clergyman, an official of the Bishop of Durham, and notorious for his extortion and ill behaviour; when he died his wife was tried for poisoning him. (She was acquitted.) Perhaps, though it is dangerous to try to guess people's motives, if Cradock had been less cantankerous and more conformist, he might not have built what was for County Durham a revolutionary house and one that must have puzzled and amazed his neighbours. See also p. 127.

THE RED HALL
Bourne, Lincolnshire

The Red Hall could well be a small manor house from its appearance, but it never was. It was built early in the seventeenth century by a local family called Fisher, whose members had only recently started calling themselves gentlemen. This was an age when correct titles were important, and the family's new status probably meant that they had acquired enough land not to have to work for their living and to warrant a certain superiority within the local community. They celebrated their arrival in the ranks of the gentry by building themselves this gentlemanly house. See also p. 151.

MERE HALL

Hanbury, Hereford and Worcester

It is unusual for houses to have been passed down from father to son through several centuries: in the course of time most families reach a generation in which there are no male heirs, and then the house passes to daughters (with a different family name) or to distant relations, or it is sold. Mere Hall, however, belonged to the Bearcroft family from the thirteenth century to the twentieth, and not only is such continuity extremely rare, it also means that in a curious way Mere is a house with no history, surrounded by none of the circumstances that have led to houses elsewhere being pulled down, altered or rebuilt. For once, the air of immemorial changelessness that people like to associate with ancient houses has some foundation in fact. See also pp. 73, 122.

HALL I'TH'WOOD

Bolton, Greater Manchester

Hall I'Th'Wood was built in the 1570s and enlarged in 1648 by Alexander Norris, who was Treasurer of the Sequestration Committee for Lancashire during the Civil War – a job that would have meant that all the forfeited property of local royalists passed through his hands. In 1899 the house was bought by the first Lord Leverhulme, restored and presented to the town of Bolton; what probably attracted the great, self-made soap millionaire to the house (besides its highly picturesque appearance and its then dilapidated state) was the fact that in the eighteenth century it had been the home of Samuel Crompton, inventor of the spinning mule – a machine that transformed the textile industry and made Crompton the personification of nineteenth-century ideals of self-improvement, inventiveness and hard work. See also pp. 133, 149.

MACKERYE END
Wheathamstead, Hertfordshire

Mackerye End was built towards the end of the sixteenth century and modernised about a hundred years later. It is not actually a manor house, but it is typical of many small estates with houses of manorial quality that grew up in the Home Counties, readily accessible from London and frequently changing hands as city fortunes came and went. Mackerye End passed through several changes of ownership from its building to 1681, when it was bought by a certain Samuel Garrard whose family retained it until 1919.

In the early nineteenth century Charles Lamb and his sister Mary were frequent visitors to Mackerye End Farm, next door; Charles apparently once began a poem that started 'Hail, Mackeray [*sic*] End!' – after which inspiration failed.

The back of Mackerye End is a pleasing, rambling assortment of extensions and outbuildings which contrast strongly with the show front on the other side. Naturally a great many houses are like this: they cannot be perpetually on parade, and provision has to be made for kennels and woodsheds and coal-cellars and potato stores and tool-sheds and well-houses and a hundred and one other ordinary needs. Almost every house in this book has buildings like this tucked away at the back to serve the everyday needs of the household.

BEVERSTONE CASTLE
Gloucestershire

An example of a castle that outlived its usefulness and became a house, Beverstone was built early in the thirteenth century on one of the many manors of the Berkeley family, whose principal house was, and still is, Berkeley Castle. It was altered more than once in the Middle Ages, and all that remains now of the medieval building is one angle tower, part ruinous and part roofed, and a small section of adjoining building which includes, for some reason that is far from clear, two chapels. The castle was severely damaged in the Civil War, suffered further fire damage in 1691, and the greater part of it is now a pleasant, comfortable, unostentatious house put up against the ruins in about 1700.

FORTON HALL
Shropshire

In the tale of its successive owners, Forton is typical of many manors. Before the Norman Conquest it belonged to a great Saxon Earl. From then it belonged to the Crown until King John made one of his nobles give him the Manor of Wolverhampton in exchange for it. Thereafter it passed through the hands of several great men, the Beauchamps, the Berkeleys, the Earls of Ormond and others, until it was bought by a lawyer, Thomas Skrymsher, in the middle of the sixteenth century, a time when new money was enabling many merchants and professional men to buy into the landed gentry. The Skrymshers' main seat was at Aqualate, elsewhere in the parish, but Forton Hall, a modest house built by them in 1665 at a cost of £100, probably stands on the ancient site of the manor house of the village.

2

THE LORD AND HIS HALL

HORHAM HALL
Nr Thaxted, Essex

Like most large houses, Horham Hall has a show front and a rear that is meant for business. At the back of the house there is a courtyard for cleaning out the kitchens and stables, for deliveries, for washing the carriage, for saddling horses, and for the other activities of the household. The house is still surrounded by a moat, and there was probably only ever one approach – by a bridge on the principal front. See also p. 63.

Life at the manor house in the Middle Ages was busy, and there would have been people everywhere – far more than in the peaceful, well-tended manor houses that remain today. To begin with, there was the lord and his family. Members of the upper classes tended to have large families, and because life expectancy was short the lord of the manor would often have inherited when his children were still quite small. So there would probably have been quite a number of children running about, as well as other members of an often extended family – such as unmarried sisters, a widowed mother, poor cousins, or others. There would also have been a large number of servants, since running a large household was a very labour-intensive business – cooking, baking, washing, cleaning, nursing, waiting on the lord of the manor and his lady and their children, constantly bringing in fuel, food and water, taking out ashes and rubbish, and looking after dogs and horses as well as people. Many lords also farmed at least part of their land, and although great men with great estates relied upon an extensive establishment of bailiffs, stewards and the like to manage their estates for them, the men who lived in the more modest manor houses included here will often have taken a personal interest in their demesne and supervised much of the work themselves. Farming was also very labour-intensive, when everything depended on ox-power, horse-power and man-power, so as well as all the household retainers there would have been a constant coming and going of farm servants to receive instructions or to bring supplies for the house.

Other villagers might also come to undertake their labour dues on the lord's lands, to pay rent or fines that the Manor Court might have imposed, or to discuss their problems as tenants or any of the many obligations to which they might find themselves liable through living on the manor. And on top of all this there will have been visits from anyone who had dealings with the lord of the manor in any of his public duties. The medieval manor house was the focus of the complex and crowded life of a still-functioning community.

The heart of the manor house was the hall, the most public part of the building, around which everything else revolved. In early manor houses the hall was the household's principal living room, supplemented only by one or two private rooms for the lord and his family's own use. The main entrance to the house led into the hall, which then usually gave access to all the other rooms of the house. It was also the largest room in the house and served all the manor's public functions and communal needs. Here the meetings of the Manor Court would be held, presided over by the lord or his steward; here the common household servants would eat, live and sometimes sleep; here, long ago, the lord of the manor himself would once have taken his meals with his followers, and he might still dine in the hall with tenants and retainers on special occasions.

In the course of time the hall came to have a superior and an inferior end (upper and lower), and at the former there was sometimes a dais where the lord sat at his high table when attending sessions of the court or while his followers and servants dined at other tables in the body of the room. In grand manor houses of the later Middle Ages there was sometimes a bay window opening off the upper end of the hall and forming an alcove that provided a degree of seclusion from the mass of other people in the hall. In many early halls there was an open fire in the middle of the floor with a vent in the roof or in one gable end; later halls were warmed by fireplaces.

In some of the earliest halls to survive, from the twelfth and thirteenth centuries, the hall was on the first floor, above store-rooms or servants' sleeping quarters, but few of these houses survive and the typical manor house of the later Middle Ages had the hall on the ground floor. Until the sixteenth century almost all these halls were open to the roof, with no floor above; such a hall could impress with its size and grandeur. This also made the hall necessarily the busiest room in the house, through which everyone had to pass to get from one end of the house to the other.

All manor houses had private rooms for the lord and his immediate family. In earlier times there was sometimes only one, known as the solar. This best room was usually on the first floor, over service rooms or over one or more rooms that could provide, for example, bedchambers for the lord's children. As time went on such private rooms became more numerous, and by the end of the Middle Ages a manor house would have one or more chambers on the first floor, leading off the hall's upper end, over a parlour on the ground floor. As yet, however, the distinction between rooms for the day and rooms for sleeping had not fully evolved, and both chambers and parlours tended to combine the functions of dining-room, sitting-room and bedroom. In some manor houses there was a private chapel, though these were rare save in the grander houses.

The service rooms included a kitchen, bakehouse, brewhouse, buttery (for keeping and serving beer – the word comes from butts, not from butter), pantry, and larders and other rooms for storing provisions. The household of the manor had to be as nearly self-sufficient as possible, and the provisioning of a large household made substantial demands on accommodation. Kitchens were sometimes detached from the rest of the house, not so much to avoid the smells (in fact one sixteenth-century writer recommended placing the kitchen where people could smell the cooking and learn how well you lived), but because of the ever-present danger of fire: with roofs that were sometimes thatched, with houses often built of timber, and with no fire-brigade but gangs of servants with buckets from the well, fire was a constant threat. The intimate connection between the house, the farm and the village was often expressed by a complex of buildings of which the manor house was just one, though the most important, and the one that gave point to all the others: the barns, stables, brewhouse, woodsheds, kennels, and all the other buildings necessary to support the economy, the pleasures and the dignity of the lord of the manor's household.

The arrangement of 'upper' and 'lower' ends meant that the medieval manor house tended to have a linear plan, but there were various ways in which this could be arranged. Houses were frequently built around a central courtyard. Sometimes one might enter this through a gatehouse opposite the hall, with family rooms on one side and service rooms on the other. Sometimes one might go straight into the hall, and find a courtyard on the far side, in which case the kitchen would usually be across the courtyard from the hall. In smaller manor houses the family rooms at the upper end and the service rooms at the lower were often placed at right-angles to the hall; this is the commonest layout of the houses in this book.

There are very many exceptions to these standard plans. There were regional preferences in these arrangements; there are, for instance, probably more small courtyard houses to be found in the west of England than elsewhere. No two houses are quite alike, and each reflects the circumstances of its location and the fashions of its time as well as the personality of its builder. But the arrangements described are typical of medieval manor houses, they were to be found everywhere, and some of them persisted long after the hall's ancient function as the centre of the life of the house had passed away.

These layouts could be found in fortified houses as well as in those that made no provision for defence. Most houses were defensible up to a point: most stood within some kind of an enclosure, sometimes entered through a separate gatehouse whose doors could be closed at night or if there were disturbances nearby; some houses, otherwise unfortified, stood within a moat. The very fact that the doors into the hall were generally the only outside doors of the house made for some degree of security. But in the wilder parts of the kingdom, particularly in the north, houses had to be built to withstand more serious assault. Such attacks might come from one's neighbours – cattle-raiding in the wild hills was almost a way of life among the northern gentry – while the unpredictable relations between England and Scotland meant that it was wise to be prepared against the depredations of a passing army, of either nation. To fortify one's house required a 'licence to crenellate', that is, to add battlements and, by implication, a strong tower; such permission was, at least in theory, restricted to men whom the king could trust not to rebel against him and whose strongholds could make a contribution to the defence of the realm. In such houses the family accommodation was often placed within a tower, into which the household and its defenders could withdraw if the need arose. Sometimes this tower alone was fortified, but sometimes all of the principal rooms, the hall included, were placed on the first floor as they were in some of the earliest surviving manor houses. The ground floor might be vaulted, for strength and for protection from fire, while for protection from enemies it would be lit only by narrow windows.

Despite these apparent differences, the layout of such fortified manor houses was often not unlike that of unfortified ones: they nearly always have a hall, with further accommodation at either end. The most striking thing is how very common these arrangements of rooms were, partly, no doubt, because they were so well suited to the kind of life that was lived in these houses. Furthermore, lords of the manor tended, almost by definition, to be conservative and probably to dislike innovation: they had an assured place to fill in society and they wanted a house that would be recognised by everyone as a familiar, suitable type of house for a man of standing. The houses that follow span a period of three hundred years, but features found in the earliest of them are still there in houses built ten generations later.

BRADLEY MANOR
Newton Abbot, Devon

Bradley is an unusual house. It was largely built in the fifteenth century, although some parts are a good deal older, and has the common manor house arrangement with the central hall flanked by rooms in gabled wings at each end. (The large window on the right lights a chapel). But the hall has a two-storey range running along the front, with more gables above it, so that the overall effect is quite different from that of most medieval manor houses: instead of the usual long roof of the hall, the house displays a fascinating, jagged outline which is accentuated by the traditional limewash of the walls. It belongs now to the National Trust. See also pp. 138, 153.

THE OLD MANOR HOUSE

Boothby Pagnell, Lincolnshire

Boothby Pagnell is one of the oldest, if not the oldest, of all complete roofed manor houses in England. It was built around the end of the twelfth century, and is a perfect example of an early form of house with the hall on the first floor. The only other room on the first floor is a solar, for the private use of the lord and his family. The ground floor is vaulted, and may have been used for storing provisions, for servants' accommodation, for stabling horses or for all three. The house would not originally have stood alone: there would also have been a number of outbuildings, including a kitchen. The principal window of the hall has been renewed, in a style later than the original.

MARKENFIELD HALL

Nr Ripon, North Yorkshire

The buildings that make up Markenfield Hall range around a courtyard, and a moat surrounds them all (the view on page 19 shows the moat and the entrance into the courtyard through the rebuilt Elizabethan gatehouse). In the far corner of the courtyard is the hall, built only a few years later than Little Wenham and quite similar to it in layout: hall, solar and chapel are all on the first floor, in an L-shaped block. Two tall, traceried windows light the hall. The kitchen is underneath, on the ground floor. The medieval chapel lies behind the three-storey Tudor building to the right of the hall.

LITTLE WENHAM HALL

Essex

Little Wenham was built between 1270 and 1290. Its appearance, that of a small castle, is deceptive and was probably intended to be – its battlements were built to impress rather than to defend. It is not strongly built; in fact it is made of brick, and is one of the earliest brick buildings in England. Little Wenham has a first-floor hall and solar and a chapel, all above a brick vaulted undercroft on the ground floor. The chapel is also vaulted, probably not so much for reasons of safety (since the hall and solar have ceilings of wood) as from a feeling that such a ceiling was appropriate to a place of worship. See also p. 104.

OLD SOAR

Plaxtol, Kent

At Old Soar the original hall has disappeared, but the late thirteenth-century first-floor solar and chapel still remain. The main ground-floor room, like the solar above it, may have been a living and sleeping room for the personal use of members of the owner's family, but there is a small room off the solar, lit only by slit windows, and other rooms beneath, whose uses are now difficult to understand. Old Soar is seven hundred years old, and people's ways of life have changed so much in their daily routines, in their attitudes to privacy, and in their material possessions, that it is not always easy to imagine how these ancient buildings were used by the households for which they were first built. Old Soar now belongs to English Heritage, and is open to the public. See also p. 105.

PURTON GREEN FARM
Stansfield, Suffolk

Purton Green Farm, the smallest house included in this book, lies in a remote corner of Suffolk. Its history is unknown: it was probably never a manor house, but it shows what many of the smallest and poorest manor houses must have looked like in the Middle Ages (it is certainly far above the sort of hovel that most peasants occupied). The hall is the lower part, and was built around 1300; the higher part is a parlour built on some 250 years later and probably replacing a solar with some other room beneath it. Outbuildings that must once have stood close to the house have vanished. The house now belongs to the Landmark Trust, which lets it as a holiday cottage, and even now one has to leave one's car a quarter of a mile away and push one's luggage to the house in a wheelbarrow.

STOKESAY CASTLE
Craven Arms, Shropshire

Stokesay Castle, in the once-troubled country on the Welsh borders, is a fortified house rather than a real castle. There are defensive towers, of which this is one, at each end of the great hall: this one has a kitchen and a well on the ground floor, and living accommodation above it. The building is in the care of English Heritage, who in 1986 began a long programme of restoration. See also pp. 65, 144, 145.

WOODSFORD CASTLE
Dorset

Like Stokesay, Woodsford Castle is less a true castle than a fortified house. It was built around the middle of the fourteenth century on land belonging to a nobleman whose main estate was in Devonshire. The house provides quite grand accommodation for the lord's occasional visits and rather less grand lodging for his retainers and for a steward who would have lived here all the year round. These rooms are all on the first floor, above stone-vaulted kitchens, store rooms, butteries and so forth at ground level. There were originally towers projecting on the far side, with no ground floor doors or windows; the side illustrated here looked onto a courtyard, so that these openings would have been protected by the courtyard's outer walls. The roof was added in the seventeenth century, when the castle became a farmhouse; it originally had a flat roof and battlements.

The central part of the castle has two doorways on the ground floor leading into two separate kitchens. The line of projecting stones (corbels) above them originally carried a lean-to roof for a covered passage to shelter servants carrying food from the kitchen to an outside stair that led to the family rooms at the left-hand end of the building. The projection to the right of these doorways contains another staircase, this one leading to lesser first-floor rooms. The pointed, Gothic windows are original; the square-headed ones are seventeenth-century alterations. See also p. 96.

THE COURT HOUSE
East Meon, Hampshire

The Court House at East Meon has lost the best rooms that originally stood at one end and retains only the hall on the right and the service rooms in the gabled wing to the left, but it remains a classic example of the commonest form of later medieval manor house – a hall with a wing at each end – of which there are several examples in this book. A survey made in 1647 listed the rooms in the house as hall, parlour, dining-room, kitchen (probably a separate building), buttery, larder, dairy, kiln (probably also external, and perhaps to make malt for beer), three lodging chambers (bedrooms), corn-chamber and cheese-chamber. By then the Court House, built in the 1390s, had probably become a farm house, but the list of rooms provides a good idea of the degree of self-sufficiency necessary in the manorial household in the Middle Ages and for some time thereafter. See also p. 17.

NORTHBOROUGH MANOR
Cambridgeshire

Northborough Manor, built around 1340, preserves its great hall virtually intact, with fine internal stone carving as well as the splendid windows visible in this view of the main front. With its two wings and its porch at one end of the hall, it is typical of what was to be a standard manor house plan, despite the fact that both wings are rebuildings of the originals. In the seventeenth century the hall was ceiled over, to provide an additional floor, hence the rather incongruous dormer window. This view of the house is framed by the arch of the gatehouse by which one approaches it from the village street. See also pp. 18, 106, 107.

OCKWELLS MANOR

Bray, Berkshire

Ockwells is a timber-framed house with a standard late medieval manor house layout: the hall is in the middle with a wing at each end; the parlour where the family probably dined every day is to the right. At the back there is a small courtyard surrounded by buildings, including the kitchen with a covered passage to protect food being carried to the hall and parlour.

Ockwells is a courtier's house, built in 1465 by John Norreys who was Usher of the Chamber and Squire of the Body of King Henry VI, and Master of the Wardrobe to Edward IV. Such posts would have brought him into everyday contact with the King, and provided plenty of opportunities for advancing his own and his friends' interests.

A great many medieval manors had barns in which to store and thresh the produce of the home farm and a dovecot for rearing pigeons, a staple meat during the winter; those at Ockwells are typical.

The Norreys family of Ockwells had been in royal service for generations, ever since in 1267 the estate had been given by the Queen, Eleanor of Provence, to her cook, Ricardo de Norreys. Coming from perhaps the most cultivated state in Europe, the Queen no doubt placed a proper importance on such things, though to be cook in a royal household was anyway a position of great responsibility.

IGHTHAM MOTE
Kent

Ightham Mote is built round a courtyard and surrounded by a moat that hugs the foot of its walls. The earliest standing remains are a hall, a chapel and two solars, all built in the 1340s. There are no surviving documents giving either the date of building or the name of its original owner, but the date was established by modern techniques of measuring the growth-rings of timbers used in the construction. In spite of its appearance of regularity, like many other old houses Ightham Mote grew by stages. A good deal of restoration and repair was carried out in the nineteenth century, but in its setting the house, which now belongs to the National Trust, remains one of the most romantic of all medieval manor houses.

The courtyard at Ightham Mote is entered through a gatehouse that has something of the air of a castle about it. The gatehouse was probably built around 1500, at a date when such entrance towers were very popular – no doubt less for their value as fortification than for their resemblance to real castles. See also pp. 95, 139.

LOWER BROCKHAMPTON

Brockhampton by Bromyard, Hereford and Worcester

This is a simple, timber-framed moated house of the fifteenth century with a gatehouse commanding its approach over the moat. One of the two wings that originally flanked the hall has been demolished, though the other still stands. The hall itself is still open, without an upper floor. Lower Brockhampton now belongs to the National Trust, and can be visited as a typical small manor house of the period. See also p. 142.

RUFFORD OLD HALL

Lancashire

The hall of the manor house built around 1500, Rufford has lost its original flanking wings but still retains a great bay window in the hall. The lantern on the roof is a somewhat fanciful nineteenth-century reconstruction of the louvre that would have let out the smoke from the fire in the centre of the hall. See also p. 26.

GREAT CHALFIELD MANOR
Nr Melksham, Wiltshire

The many windows of this splendid fifteenth-century house indicate what goes on behind them. On the left-hand side a projecting oriel window lights a fine solar on the first floor. Beneath this is an ill-lit vaulted room, perhaps some sort of secure store-room, whose window is barely visible. Next on the right is a two-storey bay, the upper floor of which is an inner closet opening off the solar, the lower floor a bay giving off the hall. Then, next to the chimney (which is proudly displayed on the main front of the house) is one of the windows of the hall. On the right-hand side is the porch, the principal entrance into the house, with an upper window that lights a minstrels' gallery at the hall's lower end. See also p. 24.

HORHAM HALL
Nr Thaxted, Essex

Horham Hall was built for Sir John Cutte, Under Treasurer to Henry VII. In the middle is the hall, with its entrance porch and great bay window. The best family rooms are in the taller gabled wing on the right; the kitchen and other service rooms are in the less prominent wing on the left. A tall staircase tower contributes further to the romantic skyline, fashionable in the early sixteenth century. There is a courtyard at the back, and there was originally another, grander one fronting the house, with wings extended further forward to enclose it. Queen Elizabeth visited Horham twice (the house as it now stands, without the buildings of the front courtyard, would have been a good deal too small for her and her retinue) and the tower may have been raised so that from there she could watch hawking in the park. See also p. 40.

ELSDON TOWER
Northumberland

Elsdon, probably built late in the fourteenth century, is typical of numerous tower houses put up by minor lords in the debateable country between England and Scotland, and is included in a list of 113 Northumberland castles made in 1415. Fortified houses elsewhere in England were an anachronism by the fifteenth century, but in the north they continued to be a necessity until in the seventeenth century the two countries were united under one crown. Although Elsdon tower bears the de Umfraville coat of arms, it was probably built not for the lord of the manor, one of the de Umfraville family, who will have had a substantial castle elsewhere, but for the parson. Like other towers, it has a stone vaulted ground floor and two living rooms above. Only in the eighteenth century did the occupants of Elsdon build a comfortable, modern house alongside the old building.

STOKESAY CASTLE
Craven Arms, Shropshire

The highly ornamental gatehouse at Stokesay was built, probably around 1600, almost entirely for show. It could hardly have kept out a serious enemy for five minutes, and in any case by that date there was no need for it to do so. But it still served the practical purpose of maintaining the privacy of the owner and his household, as well as the symbolic function of announcing his importance and (by keeping people out who had no business at the castle) proclaiming his exclusivity. See also pp. 51, 144, 145.

SANDFORD ORCAS
Dorset

A great many manor houses had gatehouses through which they were approached. The gatehouses of castles had been their first line of defence; in private houses the gatehouse did little more than provide a dignified approach to the dwelling of a man of importance. At Sandford Orcas, built in the 1550s, the gatehouse is particularly odd in that it is attached to the side of the manor house itself. There could hardly be a better demonstration of its absence of any defensive role. See also pp. 90, 114, 115.

BROUGHTON CASTLE
Oxfordshire

The gatehouse at Broughton is much more businesslike than the gatehouses of many other manor houses; it does at least command the approach to the castle across the moat. In origin it is fourteenth century, when the house itself had a semi-fortified tower at one end, but as a defensive building it was steadily downgraded, with larger windows inserted in the fifteenth century and with battlements dated as late as 1655 when they can only have been placed there (or rebuilt) for show. (The house itself became less defensible in a similar way; progressive modernisation has almost engulfed the early, fortified tower.) There was once another gatehouse commanding another bridge, but this seems to have been demolished in the eighteenth century, curiously making the house more romantically inaccessible than it would have been in the middle ages. See also pp. 2, 97, 103.

3

THE HOME OF THE SQUIRE

BECKLEY PARK
Oxfordshire

Beckley Park is not a manor house but a lodge. It was built around 1540 by Lord Williams of Thame, whose principal house was at Rycote a few miles away. Beckley was probably built for him to escape for a time from the formality of Rycote and for hunting, which is why it is so different in appearance from the conventional manor house. It has a hall, but this is on the ground floor only, with a full storey above. Its great gabled towers are nothing to do with defence, but contain a staircase, closet rooms and garderobes – lavatories – which originally discharged into the moat that rather conveniently surrounds the house. There are in fact two moats, one inside the other, and the house stands between the inner and the outer one. These moats are all that remain of an earlier castle which had fallen down by the time that Lord Williams obtained the estate. See also p. 146.

The classic manor house of the later Middle Ages had an open hall in the centre with further accommodation at each end – the lord and his family's private rooms at one end and service rooms at the other. These might be placed in line with the hall or on three or four sides of a courtyard, or most commonly, in two wings at right angles to the ends of the hall.

The sixteenth century, however, saw the transformation of the manor house. This was not a sudden change: developments in the fifteenth century were leading up to it, and it was not complete until the end of the seventeenth; but the transformation was most rapid and marked under the Tudors. The ancient hall, which had been the centre of the manor house since Saxon times, gradually became less important and the other rooms began to multiply; this led to a number of profound changes in the appearance of such houses.

The first change was the loss of the hall open to the roof, which became instead a hall on the ground floor only. This happened gradually, beginning in manorial houses soon after 1500. There were several reasons for this. First, the increasing use of chimneys to heat the hall, rather than having a louvre in the roof to let the smoke out, meant that there could be a proper ceiling which, though not as grand as a great open roof, was a good deal warmer. Next, the demand for extra space could then be met by rooms over the hall; with more rooms available, the servants no longer had to live and eat in the hall. In broader terms, the use of the hall as the centre of the communal life of the manor was gradually ceasing. As lords and their families became richer and more sophisticated they were less ready to preside over the functions and activities that once took place there. The meetings of the manor court often came to be held elsewhere, rather than in what lords of the manor increasingly regarded as their own private houses. As cash rents rather than personal services became the bond between the lord and his tenants, so there was less need – or opportunity – for them to meet or dine together. In fact, as the Middle Ages closed, the ancient hall of the manor house had very little purpose. That it survived for so long was because, even reduced in size and ceiled over, it retained a powerful symbolic and sentimental importance.

By the late seventeenth century the hall of an old manor house might still contain a few hard benches and a table as remnants of the time when servants once ate there and tenants came to the manor court, but in growing contrast to the comfortable furnishings elsewhere in the house. Servants by this time usually ate in the kitchen or in a special servants' hall. Weapons might still be hanging on the wall, relics of the days when the lord of the manor had to equip his retainers to defend the house against marauders, but by now these were little more than decoration. In grand houses the hall was ultimately superseded as a room for formal entertainment by the saloon, while in others the hall itself shrank to what in most houses it is now, the area beyond the main entrance to the house, retaining the memory of its medieval function in its name alone. These changes in the structure and function of the hall profoundly affected the outside appearance of the manor house.

Over the years manor houses had also been acquiring more rooms, though again it was in the sixteenth century that the process became most marked. There were several reasons for this, the first of which was that as the hall declined, so the need for more chambers and parlours increased. Another was the wish for exclusivity. No longer were lords satisfied with a visible position as the head of their household, their retainers and their community: it was more distinguished to set oneself apart from one's inferiors. Privacy came to be valued increasingly for its own sake, comfort was prized as much as pageantry, and taste began to be appreciated as much as mere ostentation. These changes principally concerned the inside of the house, of course, but they also affected its outside appearance: more floors, more rooms and greater comfort meant more windows and more chimneys.

A balance between the two ends of the house – the family end and the service end – began to emerge in the manor houses of the later Middle Ages, with increasing symmetry between the projecting wings flanking the hall. There was, however, a certain tension between this growing concern for regularity and the wish to distinguish one end of the house from the other. Though some houses with symmetrical fronts were being built by the middle of the sixteenth century, it was well into the seventeenth before they were more or less universal. Nonetheless, whereas in 1500 the manor house still had a clearly visible hall and solar and was as ostentatious as its owner could afford, by the middle of the seventeenth century the outside of the manor house gave little clue as to the arrangement of rooms inside, and expressed only its owner's taste and his social class. No doubt this new reluctance to flaunt one's wealth was partly a reaction to the excesses and ostentation of the Elizabethans. (A parallel change was taking place with regard to people's clothes; after the elaborate dress of the Tudors, by 1640 the fashionable colour to wear was black.) These shifts in taste reinforced the effects of the other changes that were leading to the decline of the hall.

Within this overall picture of change there were many local variations. Up-to-date fashions did not reach all parts of the country with equal speed, and there were many reasons why, even when exposed to the latest architectural ideas, people were not always willing to embrace them. In the sixteenth and seventeenth centuries people still tended to be very localised in their loyalties and outlook, and where there was still a strong local tradition of building in a certain way, those who built themselves new houses were often reluctant to stray too far from it. This was partly a question of conservatism and a preference for houses adapted to established ways of living, and partly one of self-consciousness: at a time when people's status depended (even more than today) on their perceived way of life, they were no doubt reluctant to build very revolutionary houses. Thus although these changes – the abandonment of the open hall, the multiplication of rooms and so forth – eventually became universal, there were many local variations in the manner and speed with which they were accepted.

Most of the manor houses discussed so far have been of a standard type, providing for a busy, crowded and complex community with the lord of the manor at its head. But well before the end of the Middle Ages another kind of private house, the lodge, appeared. This was not itself a manor house but was often owned and used by lords who had a manor house elsewhere. Lodges were of many sizes and functions, but a typical lodge was built for its owner on some outlying part of his estate so that he could stay there on occasional visits for hunting, for escaping for a time from the formality of life at his principal house, or if the location was more convenient for the management of that part of his property.

Life in the lodge was different from that in the manor house. There were far fewer servants, no large-scale formal entertainments, and no manor courts to be presided over. Because of this, even in the Middle Ages lodges looked different from conventional manor houses: they were usually smaller and more compact, having fewer and smaller rooms and a smaller hall. They tended to be of higher architectural quality than the houses of yeoman farmers, but were less ostentatious than manor houses. Their combination of a fairly small hall with architectural sophistication meant that they had some of the qualities that the wealthy were coming to require in the houses in which they lived all the time.

The growing number of affluent people in the sixteenth century also needed suitable houses. For a long time the manor house provided the pattern for the country houses of the rich, even if, as increasingly happened in the sixteenth and seventeenth centuries, the newly rich had no manor. These men – lawyers, professional men, and merchants – wanted the home comforts enjoyed by members of the upper classes as well as the status and the respect due to lords of the manor, and it was therefore natural for them to build the same kinds of houses. Nonetheless, from the late sixteenth century onwards these people were among the first to adopt new forms. They needed no great hall; they had few tenants or retainers, and were content to call their largest room the hall, as long as it was big enough and impressive enough to entertain a few dozen friends with honour. Particularly in the country around London where, even at this period, there were rich men living in grand houses on small estates, houses were being built with quite small halls. Furthermore, in some of these houses the hall no longer lay between the upper and lower ends of the house, as it had done in the traditional medieval manor, but in one corner of the house, or in the middle but with a whole additional range of rooms behind it. The change in layout and appearance caused by these new arrangements was enormous.

So manor houses and the houses of rich men who were not lords of the manor were now, like their owners, evolving in the same direction. Both sought to build houses with the most up-to-date amenities of fashionable living, so announcing their wealth and standing to each other and to the world.

MERE HALL
Hanbury, Hereford and Worcester

Mere carries the date 1357, but, whenever the first house on the site was built, the existing building dates from the early seventeenth century. One wing of the house is still more prominent than the other, and the original front door stood in the porch in the angle between the central range and the right wing. A later generation modernised the arrangement by putting a new front door in the middle of the central range, but the original layout remains as evidence of an earlier taste. See also pp. 34, 122.

POUNDISFORD PARK

Pitminster, Somerset

Although there was a general trend towards greater symmetry and regularity in house-building throughout England, developments took place at different speeds in different parts of the country, and Somerset in the mid-sixteenth century produced some very forward-looking houses. The tendency for houses to become more regular and symmetrical had been growing over the fifteenth century, with wings at each end of the hall increasingly balancing each other. At Poundisford, built in the 1540s, the wings are a matching pair; the entrance porch is still off-centre, but it is balanced by the hall bay. Although the hall itself is still a tall room lit by a distinctive window, it already has another floor above it. See also p. 152.

LEIGH MANOR

Winsham, Somerset

Leigh Manor carries a date of 1544, and if that is indeed when it was built it was extremely up-to-date for its time. (From its appearance one would have thought that a date in the 1570s was a good deal more likely.) The house is completely symmetrical, with no differentiation between the wings and no indication of where the hall is.

Leigh was the home of the Henley family from the Middle Ages until the 1930s, and was always known as 'the New House' – even when it was nearly four hundred years old. One suspects that this was not so much a matter of aristocratic affectation as plain conservatism: that is what the house had been called when it really had been new, and the name just stuck.

HAMBLETON OLD HALL
Leicestershire

Hambleton Old Hall was built in the early seventeenth century. One of the problems tackled by its builder was that of designing a fashionable, symmetrical façade while keeping the entrance at one end of the hall. The solution found here (and in a number of other houses of this period) was to hide the off-centre front door behind a screen. The original symmetry of the screen at Hambleton has been slightly spoiled by a later alteration. See also p. 130.

KIRSTEAD HALL
Norfolk

Kirstead Hall was built in 1614 by a successful lawyer. The windows and the wings of the house are all so nearly the same that it is only by carefully counting the panes that it is possible to differentiate one end of the house from the other, and by doing so the internal arrangements begin to be revealed. The hall, with its fourteen-pane window, is on the ground floor to the right of the porch; the best chamber is on the first floor in the right-hand wing. The rooms at the other end, where the kitchen is (its chimney is visible on the left) are lower, so there is room for an extra garret in the roof. The pediments over the windows are a classical detail that was very fashionable in East Anglia at the time. They are of brick, plastered to look like stone.

COTTERSTOCK HALL
Northamptonshire

Cotterstock assumed its present form in 1658, when it was remodelled for a certain John Norton, but it still preserves the earlier plan with wings projecting at either end, which make it look old-fashioned for its date. The ground floor windows were renewed in the eighteenth century, and would originally have had stone mullions like the ones upstairs.

In this side view of Cotterstock, the line of larger windows that zigzag up the centre of the wall marks a staircase. This is the stable and kitchen yard, with a range of outbuildings on the left and on the right a high wall to separate it from the pleasure grounds that lie beyond. The yard is now largely laid down to grass, but it would probably originally have been surfaced with stone setts or cobbles. See also p. 117.

NEWARK PARK
Ozleworth, Gloucestershire

The builder of Newark, in around 1550, was Sir Nicholas Poyntz, who had been a prominent member of Henry VIII's court in the late king's last years. Like Beckley, Newark is a lodge, built so that its owner could get away from his vast and rambling house at Iron Acton, north of Bristol, for peace and privacy. In its small and compact form, however, Newark is very different from Beckley, and also from the traditional manor house where the hall and other parts are clearly differentiated and discernible from the outside. Its hall, which was never meant for great entertainments, is indistinguishable on the outside of the house. The principal room, it is clear from the grand bay window over the front door, was the great chamber on the first floor. In many ways Newark Park was very modern for its date and looks forward to houses of the next century. See also p. 126.

ANDERSON MANOR
Dorset

Anderson Manor is an architectural masterpiece, designed by an unknown builder for John Tregonwell of Milton Abbas. It was built in 1622 on one of Tregonwell's many manors, probably for his eldest son to live in before he inherited the big house at Milton. It is four-square and up-to-date in its layout, another example where the hall ceases to be the most prominent or important room in the house. Such a plan had until recently been used only for lodges and the suburban houses of city merchants, but at Anderson it appeared in a country house of the heir of a leading county family. See also p. 113.

WHARTON COURT

Leominster, Hereford and Worcester

Wharton Court is a great square block of a house, immensely imposing when seen from a distance and no less so close to. It was built in 1604 for Richard Whitehall, a Freeman of the City of London, on a compact plan fashionable for houses being built in the country round London from the late sixteenth century. It is likely that its unusual form is the result of Whitehall's having brought London ideas down to the country with him. Wharton Court is not a manor house, since Whitehall owned no manor, but the house contains rooms of quality for a man of sophisticated tastes. The hall where lords of the manor would receive their tenantry is here no more than the largest room on the ground floor, undifferentiated in any other way. See also p. 136.

BARNHAM COURT

Sussex

Barnham was probably built in about 1640. The identity of its original owner is not known, but it was almost certainly constructed by the bricklayer-architect who built the suburban villa of the same date in London's Kew Gardens, usually called (for no very good reason) the Dutch House: the details of the brickwork and decoration are almost identical. The Dutch House was built for a City merchant, Samuel Fortry. Barnham Court is very much a suburban house of the period, and the fact that it is some sixty miles from London shows how new styles were spread both by clients who wanted up-to-date houses and by craftsmen who brought up-to-date ideas. See also pp. 119, 128.

NEWHOUSE
Goodrich, Hereford and Worcester

The late sixteenth and early seventeenth centuries were a time of architectural innovation, and the willingness to adopt new forms, which led some people to abandon the traditional manor house plan, led a few to go even further. Newhouse, built in 1636, is an extreme example of this, having three wings sticking out like the arms of a starfish. The plan is not a convenient one, which no doubt explains why there are so few other houses like it.

THORNEY ABBEY HOUSE
Cambridgeshire

The land and buildings of the great Cistercian abbey of Thorney were granted by Henry VIII to the Earl of Bedford (ancestor of the present Duke). For long it remained normal for great men to have houses on all their more substantial properties, both for occasional visits and merely to advertise their continued concern for the place, and Thorney Abbey House was built for the 5th Earl in 1660 by a local mason, John Lovin of Peterborough. Thorney Abbey House is not large, but it was very up-to-date: Lovin, the local builder, had learnt from the example of houses by London masons, and in its simplicity, symmetry and four-square plainness Thorney Abbey House looks forward to houses of the age of Wren, William and Mary and Queen Anne. See also p. 129.

HINCASTER HALL
Heversham, Cumbria

Hincaster Hall is a simple, rectangular, almost symmetrical house in a part of England that was a long way from the centres where architectural fashions were being created. The masonry is rough, the style is that of the neighbourhood, but the overall form shows that moden ideas about a house's layout and appearance had reached remote corners of England by the late seventeenth century when Hincaster was built.

FLEMINGS HALL
Bedingfield, Suffolk

Although there was a remarkable uniformity all over England in the layout of manor houses, there were also local variations. Flemings Hall, built around 1550, is a good example of a type of house popular in Norfolk and Suffolk in the sixteenth and early seventeenth centuries. Here, although the rooms themselves are the same as those found in any other house of the same class – a hall in the middle, family rooms at one end and service rooms at the other – they are all laid out in a straight line rather than in wings at right angles to the central range. The hall is on the ground floor only.

WOOD LANE HALL
Sowerby, Yorkshire

Wood Lane Hall, built in 1649, is a good example of type of house to be found in the Yorkshire Pennines. By the standards of the south of England it is quite extraordinarily old fashioned, yet it shows how strong regional traditions and differences still were in the seventeenth century. It still has projecting wings at either end of the hall, it still has an off-centre porch into the low end and, strangest of all, it still has an open hall at least a century after smart houses elsewhere were acquiring halls on the ground floor only. Although Wood Lane Hall is a particularly good example of its type, there are dozens of similar houses in the area, and it is clear that such features, long superseded in other parts of the country, still seem to have embodied for Yorkshire clothiers the ideal of the gentlemanly house. See also pp. 112, 124, 140.

NAAS HOUSE
Lydney, Gloucestershire

Naas House is a late representative of another local house type: the country houses of the Bristol and Gloucestershire clothiers in the seventeenth century. These are flat-fronted and gabled, and form a distinct group in the prosperous countryside north of Bristol. Naas is an outlying example on the other side of the river Severn. The little prospect room on top – sometimes called a lantern or belvedere – is a feature often found in late-seventeenth-century manor houses and the houses of men of similar wealth and status, and many more houses probably had them once: they are apt to rot if not properly looked after and then are usually removed. The lantern at Naas House may have served not only for admiring the view, but also for the owner to watch for his ships coming up the river.

SANDFORD ORCAS
Dorset

Sandford Orcas was built around the middle of the sixteenth century. The hall is at one end, with identical mullioned windows lighting it and the great chamber above it. To the rear there is a small courtyard, with the kitchen on the far side. In some ways Sandford Orcas is old-fashioned: it is quite assymetrical, and the way in which the hall is positioned at one end rather than in the middle harks back to some much earlier medieval houses. A number of Tudor houses in the west of England share this layout, however, which obviously remained acceptable among west country gentry when it was less so elsewhere. But, in that the hall has a fine great chamber over it – a room at least equally grand – Sandford Orcas is a modern house for its date. See also pp. 66, 114, 115.

DUTTON HALL
Lancashire

This is another Pennine hall, built in the 1670s by Richard Townley whose family had owned Dutton since the fourteenth century. Their overlords were the Sherbornes of Stoneyhurst, to whom they paid an annual rent of one red rose.

Dutton Hall is another house old-fashioned for its date, even though it does have a ground-floor hall with the best chamber on the first floor. The entrance is off-centre, and the bay window of the hall and the chamber occupies almost the whole of the front of the house. There is a balcony on top, from which to admire the view – a feature that in one form or another was becoming popular at the time. (The look-out or belvedere at Naas House, p. 89, is another version of the same theme.)

NORTH LEES HALL
Hathersage, Derbyshire

Perhaps to enhance the glories of their own time, people in the reign of Elizabeth I liked to identify themselves with past glories. Medieval romances were written and widely read, ideals of chivalry were revived (even though there had not been a great deal that was idealistic about the actual behaviour of many medieval knights and barons), and some houses were built to resemble fairy-tale castles. North Lees Hall was one such, though on a fairly modest scale, with its flat roof and battlements.

OWLPEN MANOR
Dursley, Gloucestershire

Owlpen has both a memorable position and a memorable name. Its position, next to the church, is clearly an ancient one. Its name is slightly less ancient, sadly having nothing to do with owls but deriving from the fact that it was the home of the Oldpen family in the Middle Ages.

Like many other houses, Owlpen Manor has been partially rebuilt at various times, so that throughout successive alterations it has preserved its medieval plan even though very little of the original house remains. The central part of the house is a sixteenth-century rebuilding of the hall; on the left, the solar was in its turn rebuilt in 1611. In the seventeenth century a separate, free-standing meeting-room for the manor court was built: the lord of the manor clearly no longer wanted these meetings to be held in his home.

FYFIELD MANOR
Oxfordshire

Higher standards of living meant that a great many manor houses were partly but not entirely rebuilt in the sixteenth and seventeenth centuries: many people sensibly felt that there was no point spending money on a completely new house if parts of the old one could still serve a useful purpose. Fyfield is a medieval manor house partly modernised in just such a way. On the left is the solar block, built of timber probably around 1400, and at the centre is the entrance porch of the same date which led into the hall in the usual way. The hall range itself, however, was rebuilt in stone around 1600, on three floors and with a fashionable display of gables. The result is a marvellous pattern of triangles and rectangles of different colours and materials. See also p. 25.

IGHTHAM MOTE
Kent

This view illustrates the unintentional result of successive alterations. It is sometimes tempting to condemn as insensitive such changes as these – for instance, the way in which, in the eighteenth century, a classical Venetian window was stuck in the middle of a Tudor gable – but here the effect is the creation of a great richness of textures and patterns. Furthermore, besides their visual attractiveness, such changes are historical evidence for changes in architectural fashions and in the standards of living of a house's successive owners. See also pp. 58, 59, 139.

WOODSFORD CASTLE
Dorset

The original, medieval hall window at Woodsford Castle was restored in the nineteenth century, but above it are a rectangular window (now bricked-in), added in the seventeenth century when the hall was subdivided, and above that another window added in the eighteenth century, when an attic floor was inserted. The stone bracket to the left of the bricked-in window was to support wooden bratticing – a temporary platform that could be built out from the face of the battlements at need in order to give greater protection to the walls beneath and make it harder for enemy to approach them. See also pp. 52, 53.

BROUGHTON CASTLE
Oxfordshire

Light pours from one side of the house to the other through the old glass of the great Tudor windows of the hall. On the first floor the central window lights the great chamber over the hall. This window probably dates from the 1550s, with Renaissance pilasters (which were very up-to-date for the time) forming the mullions. See also pp. 2, 67, 103.

4

BUILDING FOR SHOW

YELFORD MANOR
Oxfordshire

Yelford Manor began as a house with a one-storey open hall, and, like a very great many other medieval houses (Northborough, for instance, p. 55), was modernised by the insertion of a floor above the hall. At Yelford there is very little evidence of this on the outside, but there is a fine bay window to light the hall and the chamber above it, which was probably added when this flooring-in was carried out. The upper floors of the wings project forward to form jetties. There is no particular structural reason for this feature, though obviously it can only be done when a house is at least grand enough to have an upper floor. It is usually only the main fronts of timber houses that are jettied, probably largely for show. See also pp. 15, 141.

The appearance of the manor house was not dictated solely by its layout and use. What was of more concern to the people who built them was that their decoration should adequately reflect their own wealth, status and standard of living. Every landowner wanted to live in a house appropriate to his social standing, not so much because of a desire to overawe his inferiors but more through a sense of what was due to his own position in society. Added to this was the wish to confirm his position in the eyes of his peers.

The Middle Ages set much store by appearances. Living was very public, and authority and status were expressed with a good deal of ceremonial. The forces of authority, such as they were, sought to impose their power as much by parading their importance as by actually enforcing the law. Noblemen maintained vast retinues for display rather than for any practical service (though supporting the dignity of one's lord was considered an important service in itself). They dined in public, with plate displayed on the sideboard and their food brought in in procession. Rules of heraldry were formalised, and men were jealous of their titles, of correct degrees of precedence and of their coats of arms. Even in death the funerals of the great were occasions for exaggerated grief, panoply and pomp. Above all, men were concerned for their honour, which subsisted in a complex code of personal loyalties and public display. In a society which judged so much by appearances, it was natural for men of importance to show it in their houses. The manor house was the physical embodiment of the values of the society that created it.

This is partly why the great hall of the medieval manor house was so prominent; over and above its size, it was the heart of the lord of the manor's authority over his household and the community, and it was considered appropriate that it should be highly visible. The same is true of many other features: the prominence given in many houses to the solar, for instance, whether by means of its architectural decoration or by its position and size, or the presence of an elaborate gatehouse, which in many houses was not so much a defensive structure as a way of formally marking the approach to the house of a man of standing. In some grand medieval houses a great, detached kitchen had a lofty roof which did more than provide ventilation for the heat and smoke: it also announced to the world that this was the home of a man who lived well and entertained lavishly. The layout of a medieval house was meant to be read from the outside: the parts of a house had a visible meaning over and above their actual, practical functions.

Besides the lavish use of building materials, by which the owner of a manor house could demonstrate his wealth to all beholders, there were many architectural elements that could be used tellingly for the same purpose. Windows were among the most expressive of these. Window glass first became common in rich men's houses in the fourteenth century, but for a long time windows commonly had glazing in the top only, with shutters at the bottom to be opened on warm days, or at least when the wind was coming from the opposite direction. However, the growing availability of glass made larger windows that let in more light increasingly practicable, and by the end of the sixteenth century windows were sometimes very large indeed. In early manor houses the largest and most elaborate windows were those of the lord's great hall, showing it off to the world. If the hall had an oriel, a feature that became increasingly common for as long as the one-storey open hall persisted, this usually projected on the principal front of the house, again proclaiming the lord's wealth and high living. The windows of the solar were originally relatively small, though usually with some decoration; by the fifteenth century these, too, were becoming larger and more ostentatious. By the sixteenth century large, glazed windows throughout the house made another point: that its owner could afford to warm every room in his house, despite the great expanse of glass and even in the depths of winter.

Chimneys were another feature that evolved with the passage of time. In the earliest manor houses the hall was usually the only heated room, and only if it was on an upper floor was there commonly a chimney and a fireplace; otherwise, the hall was heated by an open fire in the middle of the floor. An open fire was inefficient and smoky, and though it provided some warmth to the generality of people in the hall, it provided no special benefit for the lord himself. Fireplaces in ground floor halls began to be common from the end of the fourteenth century, those in solars and other family rooms in the fifteenth, and as chambers multiplied and standards of comfort rose, an increasing number of other rooms were provided with fireplaces. Rare, early chimneys were often decorated; by the fifteenth and sixteenth centuries chimney stacks were frequently highly ornamented and became one of the most prominent forms of display, soaring above the roof-line in a forest of spiralling brick or stone.

There were other ways of enhancing the silhouette of the house. Gables were another structural feature upon which expense could be effectively lavished and, like fine windows, they often marked the best rooms of the house. From the fifteenth century, particularly in the eastern counties, the gables of brick and stone houses were often given a decorative outline. These sometimes took the form of a series of steps – creating 'crow-step' gables, as they are often called – or, from the late sixteenth century and through much of the seventeenth, they appeared as a series of highly decorative steps and curves. These are often called Dutch gables, but although it is true that ornamental gables were fashionable in contemporary Holland and Flanders, differences in their shapes show that English invention did not owe much to foreign patterns.

The limitations of timber construction meant that the gables of wooden houses could not be given spectacular silhouettes, but they could be given richly carved 'barge boards' under the eaves. The appearance of timber houses could also be enhanced by means of elaborate framing. In these framing patterns local styles naturally predominated, but a feature common to many superior timber buildings was the projecting upper floor or 'jetty'. This practice is so familiar that popular images of picturesque old houses almost invariably include at least one half-timbered building with a jettied front. The origin of the feature is not known; various theories have been put forward, none of them very satisfactory, but what is certain is that it provided a splendid means of display: the projecting timbers could be carved and window bays incorporated, while the forward and upward thrust of the structure is impressive in itself.

The period of greatest flamboyance in domestic architecture was probably the early sixteenth century, although many Elizabethan houses make a great display of architectural virtuosity. But the grandest Elizabethan houses were the homes of the aristocracy, men who played a great part in public life and in affairs of state, and who still owed it to their position to make a great show of their importance. Meanwhile, changes were taking place in all the houses of the upper classes. These were the result of an increasing desire for privacy and for comfort, a growing awareness of taste and luxury as measures of a man's status and a corresponding tendency to make a show inside the house rather than outside. For a time the aristocracy still lived very publicly, but by the early seventeenth century the homes of lords of the manor and their peers were beginning to look rather less ostentatious than they had done a couple of generations earlier.

However, although the exterior of the manor house was becoming less ostentatious, its appearance was still very important. There was an increasing striving for regularity and symmetry, combined with a growing use of new architectural styles – the classical ornament of the Renaissance. It is likely that the new fashion in decoration was at first a matter of prestige rather than of taste; among its first patrons were members of the Court circle of Henry VIII and his immediate successors, and these were very much men to emulate. But it is also likely that as classical education became more widespread, classical architectural detail began to be appreciated for its own sake. By the early seventeenth century some knowledge of architecture – which effectively meant knowing something about the classical orders – was coming to be regarded as a desirable part of a gentleman's education.

The new decorative style can be seen as a substitute for the ostentatious ornament of the previous generation: it was becoming smarter to demonstrate sophistication and knowledge and to reject mere, vulgar display. But such an approach depended on education, on contact with up-to-date thinking, and on not being influenced by other people who might not themselves have such advanced ideas about architecture. In the end the new ideas and new taste won the day, and gradually evolved into the plainness, regularity and erudition of Georgian building; but this process took a very long time.

BROUGHTON CASTLE
Oxfordshire

Although chimneys, windows and other details were often designed so as to draw attention to the dignity of a house's owner or to the luxury of the house itself, some of the features of the manor house that can be read from the outside were also purely functional. In this category is the little sixteenth-century garderobe (lavatory) that projects from the upper part of the walls of Broughton Castle. It is set among an extraordinary variety of windows which are evidence of the numerous alterations that the house has undergone. See also pp. 2, 67, 97.

LITTLE WENHAM HALL
Essex

In medieval manor houses the importance of different rooms was often marked by windows of differing degrees of elaboration. These thirteenth-century windows at Little Wenham mark the hall, on the left, and the chapel, on the right, while beneath the latter is a narrow slit window of the vaulted undercroft: here, on the ground floor, security was more important than light. See also p. 48.

OLD SOAR
Plaxtol, Kent

As at Little Wenham, the most elaborate window of Old Soar marks the chapel on the left. Old Soar could not have been defended against serious attack, but its occupants were equipped to repel marauders: the garderobe at the right and the rooms on the ground floor are lit only by arrow-slits, designed to give defenders a good field of view but to make things difficult for an enemy. See also p. 49.

NORTHBOROUGH MANOR
Cambridgeshire

The fourteenth-century windows of the hall have above them the dormer window of the attic floor which was inserted in the seventeenth century. In the 1970s the inserted floor was removed, restoring the open hall to its original form, but the dormer window was retained as evidence of a period in the house's history.

In the Middle Ages only the grandest houses, or those with halls on the first floor (where open fires would be dangerous) had chimneys, and when they did they were generally decorated in a manner appropriate to a feature so rich and rare. The fourteenth-century hall chimney at Northborough is of stone, six-sided, with a decorated top and tracery carved round the base. See also pp. 18, 55.

BARLBOROUGH HALL
Derbyshire

Windows of houses were becoming larger and plainer throughout the sixteenth century, and the windows of Barlborough, built in the 1580s, with straight heads and uniform shapes and sizes, exemplify this development. They are also typical of their period in taking up so much of the wall surface: in some houses of the late sixteenth and early seventeenth centuries there seems to be more window than wall. See also p. 31.

CONISTON OLD HALL
Cumbria

Evening light catches the four great chimneys of Coniston in the Lake District. These impress by their size rather than by their decoration: to have a house with four hearths in so remote a part of England was a rare distinction in the sixteenth century, and one to advertise. See also p. 22.

EAST BARSHAM MANOR
Norfolk

Multiplication of fireplaces produced a multiplication of chimneys – in fact, some houses were built with fake stacks to look as though there were more heated rooms than there actually were. When houses were built on compact plans and with upper floors it became possible to place fireplaces back-to-back and above or below one another in the same wall. In this way several flues could be built together, leading up to an impressive cluster of chimneys. Clustered chimney stacks, such as those at East Barsham, first appeared late in the fifteenth century; until then, fireplaces were not common enough even in great houses to make such massing as this possible. The stacks of East Barsham are among the most impressive of early Tudor chimneys and do much to provide the house with its dramatic roof-line.

The enormous Royal Arms over the gateway at East Barsham proclaim the family's loyalty to the Crown and the glory of the Tudor royal house. The early sixteenth century was the period when great country houses were probably at their most flamboyant, and though East Barsham is neither the greatest nor the most highly decorated, it is a fine example of the fashion of its time. See also pp. 1, 27, 118, 147.

WOOD LANE HALL
Sowerby, West Yorkshire

The initials of John Dearden and his wife, for whom Wood Lane Hall was built, and the date of their fine new house are proudly displayed over the front door. Putting one's initials and the date of construction on one's house had been popular at the highest levels of building in the sixteenth century; by the middle of the seventeenth the practice had rather gone out of fashion with the smartest people, but continued to be popular for some time in less elevated circles. John Dearden was a self-made clothier. See also pp. 88, 124, 140.

ANDERSON MANOR
Dorset

The arms of John Tregonwell, for whom Anderson Manor was built, contains three Cornish choughs (the family originally came from Cornwall), and the birds decorating this lead rainwater-head must be some of them. Other leadwork at the house has the full coat of arms, Tregonwell's initials and the date. The dating and decorating of such leadwork continued long after other forms of personal labelling had passed out of fashion: it is always worthwhile looking at the rainwater goods of a seventeenth or eighteenth century country house to see if they carry dates or initials. See also p. 81.

SANDFORD ORCAS
Dorset

Sandford Orcas was built in the 1550s by the Knoyle family, who placed over the front door their own arms impaling those of another gentry family, the Frys of Iwerne, who lived some fifteen miles away (although the arms themselves are now no longer visible on this shield). There is a slight mystery about this; to arrange coats of arms in this way – half one family's, half another's – generally indicates a marriage, yet there is no record of such an alliance having taken place. Perhaps it was intended or anticipated and never happened.

The peaks of the gables at Sandford Orcas are guarded by little heraldic lions carrying coats of arms. These coats of arms can hardly be seen from the ground, but they convey an appropriate impression of grandeur. See also pp. 66, 90.

BASSINGTHORPE MANOR
Lincolnshire

Every architectural device was used to give Bassingthorpe an interesting roofscape: the paired chimneys are treated as pillars, the attic window is embellished with a classical pediment, and the gable has crow-steps. See p. 28 for a more general view of the house.

COTTERSTOCK HALL
Northamptonshire

The porch of Cotterstock has a highly decorative gable, set between dormer windows with an attractive outline. There is a small balcony just beneath it, a popular feature in many seventeenth-century manor houses (Dutton Hall, Lancashire, has another version – see p. 91). Bands of stone, or strapwork, decorate the gable. The style first appeared late in the sixteenth century and for a time was immensely popular, but by 1658 when Cotterstock was built, it was already going out of fashion. See also pp. 78, 79.

EAST BARSHAM MANOR
Norfolk

Finials of one sort or another are a common decorative feature of sixteenth-century houses, and these large ones on the roof of East Barsham Manor add to the general exuberance of its architecture. See p. 00, for the chimneys of East Barsham, and pp. 1, 27, 110, 111, 147.

BARNHAM COURT
Sussex

This rear view of Barnham Court displays a riot of Dutch gables, crow-step gables and chimney stacks. See also pp. 83, 128.

S
E

GRAVETYE MANOR

Nr East Grinstead, Sussex

For most people local fashions in building were until fairly recently more important than national ones: it was more important to keep up with the neighbours than to build a house which, however up-to-the-minute, would look out of place in the neighbourhood. Furthermore, local fashions naturally depended on local knowledge, and new trends took a long time to travel. There was a very widespread fashion for gabled fronts to houses around 1600 (when Gravetye was built), but the way in which this fashion was realised varied very much from place to place. Gravetye's gables run along the skyline like those of many manor houses of the period, but in detail their design reflects that of other houses of the immediate area. See also p. 29.

GULLEGE

Nr East Grinstead, Sussex

Gullege is a mile or two across the valley from East Grinstead, and the way in which its gables imitate those of the grander Gravetye Manor suggests that its builder was trying to make the same kind of impression. See also p. 150.

MERE HALL
Hanbury, Hereford and Worcester

The central range of Mere Hall has a line of small gables, which have absolutely no practical use (it would have been easier to have built the roof without them) but which greatly enhance the appearance of the house. There are several other houses in the area of Mere Hall, built around 1600, with similar gablets forming a saw-edge against the sky. See also pp. 34, 73.

MIDDLE BEAN HALL
Bradley Green, Hereford and Worcester

Middle Bean Hall is not far from Mere (in the previous picture) and the gables of its top storey are so similar that their owners clearly shared the same architectural tastes.

WOOD LANE HALL
Sowerby, West Yorkshire

The seventeenth-century houses of the rich clothiers of Yorkshire are among the most distinctive of all regional groups: in their details many of them closely resemble each other and are remarkably unlike anything else. A strong regional building tradition was clearly still very much alive in the area and continued to satisfy the aspirations of the local élite. Round windows on entrance porches, such as can be seen at Wood Lane Hall, are a distinctive feature of many of these Yorkshire houses. See also pp. 88, 112, 140.

NEW HALL
Elland, West Yorkshire

New Hall is another highly idiosyncratic West Yorkshire house, with the typical round window in the porch. See also pp. 11, 148.

NEWARK PARK
Ozleworth, Gloucestershire

When the new decorative style of the Renaissance first reached England it was used mostly for small details. It was over a century before it began to be appreciated that classical architecture comprised a complete and highly sophisticated set of rules for architectural composition, as well as simply decoration that reminded people of the ancient world. The front door of Newark Park, with its Tuscan columns and classical pediment, is an astonishingly learned piece of work for its date (*c.* 1550). See also p. 80.

GAINFORD HALL
Durham

The front door of Gainford, built in 1600, typifies the treatment of classical architecture in the sixteenth and early seventeenth centuries. There are classical columns beside the porch, but they now carry a great top-hamper of decoration and flank a highly ornamented doorway, suggesting rather more what people thought the ancient Romans ought to have done than what they actually did. This is decoration seeking to impress by its lavishness rather than by its erudition. See also p. 32.

BARNHAM COURT

Sussex

The brick front of Barnham Court, probably built around 1640, shows its builder displaying rather more knowledge of classical architecture than many of his predecessors did (though it is still somewhat idiosyncratic). The house (of which there is a general view on p. 83) has a front door with a pediment, a good classical cornice and rows of pilasters along the wall both upstairs and down. Such pilasters were particularly popular with builders in the London area at the time, and were probably suggested by an Italian textbook like that of Sebastiano Serlio, which was translated into English in 1611 and has several designs for buildings with rows of pilasters one above the other. See also p. 119.

THORNEY ABBEY HOUSE

Cambridgeshire

The front door of Thorney Abbey House, built in 1660, looks unremarkable, because by the standards of later architecture there is nothing unusual about it. But at the time it was still quite sophisticated for a provincial builder to put up so plain and correct a classical doorway. Thorney Abbey House was a harbinger of things to come. See also p. 85.

5

STRUCTURE AND MATERIALS

HAMBLETON OLD HALL
Leicestershire

The classical screen that links the two wings of Hambleton, giving a touch of architectural sophistication to what is otherwise a very traditional house, is executed in a local Jurassic limestone. This is one of the best building stones, found and used from Dorset to Lincolnshire, lasting well (when away from industrial pollution and if chosen with care – the old quarrymen generally knew which beds were the most durable) and capable of carrying fine, crisp detail. See also p. 78.

Manor houses tended to be very uniform in their layout. However, they were remarkably varied in their choice of building materials and the way in which these materials were used. Most of the great Anglo-Saxon halls that have been excavated were of timber rather than stone; but among the oldest manor houses to have survived, from the late twelfth and thirteenth centuries, are houses of both stone and timber. Stone was almost everywhere a prestige building material, but very substantial timber houses could last as long and be equally impressive, and builders sometimes preferred it because of the rich decorative effects that could be achieved by using it. Late in the Middle Ages, brick was increasingly used in building for the elite. But the choice of materials for the manor house invariably depended upon the same considerations: the need for strength and permanence, the availability of local materials, and the desire to make a show.

The variety of types of building stones is enormous and each gives a house a different character as well as affecting its relationship to the landscape around it. Such stones differ in colour, in texture, and in the ease with which they may be worked. Hardest of all are the granites, used mostly in south-west England, though occurring in some areas of the Midlands and Cumbria. Granite walls tend to be massy and stone carving rough, and it is tempting to suppose that the often small size of granite houses was the result not only of poverty, but also of the sheer difficulty of working the material. Other intractable stones are the flints and cherts (rather similar to flint), used mostly in the south-east and East Anglia, which are small, knobbly and intensely hard. Their small size means that walls built of them are not very strong, their shape makes laying them difficult, while their hardness makes them almost impossible to cut and wholly impossible to carve. In areas where flint was used, stone or brick was generally employed for angles and mouldings, even if this meant the expense of bringing in better stone from elsewhere. The contrast of texture between these hard materials and more easily worked stones was sometimes exploited for particular decorative effects. Some stones, most notably chalk, make poor buildings by virtue of their softness. There is a broad band of chalk stretching from Dorset, through Wiltshire and Berkshire, north-east through the Chilterns and eastward to Kent, within which, however, there are areas of sufficiently hard chalk to be used for buildings of a very distinctive whiteness.

The best building stones are the sandstones and limestones. Limestones occur in a great sweep from Somerset and Dorset, through Gloucestershire, to Northamptonshire and Lincolnshire, and also in the Pennines. Those of the south are some of the loveliest of all building stones, often described as honey-coloured, golden or creamy. Famous limestones include Portland from Dorset (almost white in colour), Chilmark from Wiltshire, Ham Hill from Somerset, Bath from Somerset and Gloucestershire, Taynton from Oxfordshire, and Ketton, Barnack, Clipsham and Ancaster from Northamptonshire and Lincoln. Though broadly similar, these limestones have their own local character. They are all, however, easy to carve when fresh from the quarry, and they have been used since the Middle Ages for some of the finest architectural detail. The northern limestones, from Derbyshire, Yorkshire and County Durham, are rather different. They tend to be greyer and less easy to work, but their more sombre shades and harder texture seem in tune with the harsh upland landscape. The limestones also include those appropriately known as ragstones (such as the Kentish Rag of London and the south-east and the Coral Rag of parts of Oxfordshire), which are difficult to work and have only been used in the local absence of anything better.

Sandstones are more varied still, with stone of different colour sometimes occurring in the same layer of the same quarry. The West Midlands include a broad belt of red sandstones from Gloucestershire north to Cheshire, with stones from different places weathering very differently and producing very different effects. In colour they range from pale yellowish-orange to an almost liver-coloured red. The sandstones of the North Midlands, of which Mansfield produced some of the best, are some of the finest of all building stones and some of the most variable in hue. The Hornton stone of North Oxfordshire and Warwickshire is another multi-coloured stone, with patches of greyish or greenish-blue. Some of the northern sandstones are very coarse in texture and are known as gritstones; these are immensely durable, resistant to fine carving, and seem to suit the northern character. There are poor sandstones just as there are poor limestones, typically in Surrey, Sussex and Norfolk; some of these are durable enough, but difficult to cut and harder still to carve, and often occur only in narrow

HALL I'TH'WOOD
Bolton, Greater Manchester

This is a typical example of the extravagant use of woodwork of the north in the late sixteenth century. It is not certain why northern framing was generally so much more elaborate and inventive than southern styles, but it may simply be because large houses in the north continued to be built of wood for longer than in the south, where timber was increasingly being replaced by brick. On the other hand, local taste must have been an important influence, and local taste defies easy explanation. See also pp. 35, 149.

beds furnishing small pieces. While most limestones are pleasing (or at least not unattractive) there exist sandstones whose colour can be positively disagreeable.

Poorer building stones were often covered up with a render made of thick lime plaster. The resulting effect can be most attractive (though it was for weather-proofing as much as for appearance) and, provided the right materials are used, it is a treatment still to be recommended. A lime wash, sometimes coloured, was also traditionally applied to timber-framed buildings in some parts of England, and this, too, if regularly renewed is an excellent way of protecting woodwork of a quality too poor to be worth displaying.

The alternative to stone for buildings of quality was timber. Good timber was sometimes hard to get – demand for building timber had always to compete with a need for fuel – but it was generally available to those who could afford it. The preferred timber for building was oak, worked green, when the wood was still full of sap and easy to cut: seasoned oak is difficult to work and needs the sharpest tools. One reason why so many old timber houses are so distorted is that they were built before the wood was seasoned and it dried out in place, twisting as it did so. Timbers were roughly sized by splitting and then squared up with a side-axe. The space between them was traditionally filled with wattle and plaster, and increasingly, from the sixteenth century onwards, with brick. (Incidently, stories about houses being made of ships' timbers are invariably myths: one has only to think of the labour of hauling great timbers dozens of miles across country and then working them, unsuitable in shape and rock-hard with age, into a quite different structure to realise how impractical it would have been.)

The range of visual effects created by different styles of timber framing was almost as great as that in stone, and there is a great deal of variation in the patterns of timber framing employed from one part of the country to another. Timber afforded great scope for conspicuous consumption – for parading one's wealth by using more than was structurally necessary. In some areas a fashionable extravagance was to place the uprights of the frame very close together. It was always necessary to brace a timber-framed building with diagonal members, and though in the south-east these diagonal braces are sometimes partly hidden (so as not to detract from the effect of these ranks of close-set uprights), elsewhere they lent themselves to a great variety of decorative forms. In the west, the more common tradition of framing was with rectangular panels, and in rich men's houses these tended to be small and often filled with short cross-braces arranged in complex repeated patterns. In some extreme cases in the north-west, in Cheshire and Lancashire, such panels can be so small and so filled with decoration, as to make them almost solid wood. And wherever wood was used it could be carved into ornament.

When brick was first used it was in those regions where there was no satisfactory building stone – down the east coast, in the south-east and East Anglia. The early appearance of brick in these areas may have been suggested by its use across the North Sea, for medieval brickwork is common in the Low Countries, in Germany and the Baltic. Wherever possible, bricks were made on site: the brickmaker would hope to find a suitable clay and wood to fire it as close to the new building as possible, to save the cost of transport. The earliest brick manor house in this book, Little Wenham (p. 48) is of the thirteenth century, but it was another two hundred years before brick began to be used at all widely, and then only for prestige buildings. Its appeal, besides its strength and its novelty, was its colour and its decorative potential. From the fifteenth century onwards brick was increasingly used ornamentally: patterns on walls were easily made by using a combination of red and black bricks, and brick embellishments can be made easily and cheaply using moulds. When Renaissance ornament first appeared in England early in the sixteenth century on the houses of the rich, following the fashions of Italy, France and the Low Countries, brick houses were among the first to display it.

In some buildings stone, timber and brick were used in combination with each other. Stone was sometimes introduced for the dressings of brick houses, for example for door and window surrounds, and for corner-stones – quoins – where stone was desirable for strength. A second reason for combining the two was taste. When brick first became fashionable (at different times in different places) it might be used for the more prominent parts of a house, stone for the parts that were less visible. As time passed and brick became more common and consequently less desirable, some parts of brick houses might be dignified by being made of stone, or houses might be faced in stone over a basically brick structure. Stone and timber sometimes appear together when a house originally built of timber has been partly rebuilt in stone, when this has become the fashionable material to use or when an owner could afford to update part of his house but not to rebuild it entirely. Furthermore, whereas timber framing was originally filled with plaster and wattle, from the fifteenth century onwards timber panels were often filled with brick, with the bricks sometimes laid in patterns. That this was a question of taste rather than being simply for greater strength is shown by cases where plaster has been painted to imitate brickwork.

WHARTON COURT
Leominster, Hereford and Worcester

The classical porch of Wharton Court was added to the house in the 1660s. It is built of the New Red sandstone that occurs from Devonshire north through the western counties as far as Cumbria. In this great stretch of country there are many variations in the stone, but it is never among the hardest of building stones, and the variety that was available locally to the builders of Wharton Court has not weathered well, despite relative freedom from pollution in that rural area. See also p. 82.

NAPPA HALL
Askrigg, West Yorkshire

Nappa is in the north-west corner of Yorkshire, beneath the spectacular crags of Carboniferous limestone which rim the northern slopes of Wensleydale and which furnished the material for Nappa Hall itself. The stone is less easily worked than the younger limestones of the south, but has a stern beauty of its own. See also p. 16.

BRADLEY MANOR
Newton Abbot, Devon

The chapel at Bradley, situated in one of the wings of the house, is approached by a passage room on the ground floor. This antechapel (to give it its correct name) has windows whose stone hoods are ornamented with carvings of the signs of the Evangelists: this curious creature is the lion of St. Mark, carved by someone who certainly had never seen a lion. Originally it was painted in various colours. One is so used to the bare stonework of medieval buildings, after centuries of wind and rain have washed off all the paint, that it is difficult to visualise the bright, sometimes crude, colouring that was common on buildings in the middle ages. See also pp. 45, 153.

IGHTHAM MOTE
Kent

The picture shows a detail of the hall door at Ightham Mote. Ightham is part-stone, part-timber; an incentive to use timber must have been, to some extent at least, the poor quality of the local stone, the Kentish Rag, which does not lend itself to fine work. The stones of the walling are no more than roughly squared up; to do anything much better with the intractable ragstone was almost impossible before the advent in the nineteenth century of power-driven masonry saws. See also pp. 58, 59, 95

WOOD LANE HALL
Sowerby, Yorkshire

The Yorkshire gritstones are hard and coarse-textured, and their recalcitrant quality probably contributed to the creation of the crude, almost barbaric, detail that is characteristic of houses of the area. On the other hand its uniformity of texture makes it possible to quarry it in large blocks. If there is any dirt in the air (as there so often is in the industrial districts of Yorkshire) the stone weathers to a sooty black, but it is relieved at Wood Lane by fine, whitish lines of mortar. See also p. 88, 112, 124.

YELFORD MANOR
Oxfordshire

Yelford is a good example of a style of timber framing popular in the south and east of England, known as 'close studding': the upright timbers in the wall are close together, much closer in fact than is really necessary to hold the building up. Because of the disappearance of almost all fifteenth- and sixteenth-century peasant houses, it probably makes less of an impression now than it did at the time, when this prodigal use of building materials would have contrasted starkly with the hovels of the ordinary villagers on the manor. See also pp. 15, 98.

LOWER BROCKHAMPTON
Brockhampton by Bromyard, Hereford and Worcester

Two different styles of timber framing are here exemplified in one house. The walls of Lower Brockhampton are partly framed with closely spaced studs (the upright members) and partly with the square panels generally more popular in the west. On the right, at the rear of the house – which is otherwise mainly of the fifteenth and sixteenth century – is an addition typical of the final, expiring use of wood in the early eighteenth century, with very slender timbers and large areas of brick in between. See also p. 60.

HASLINGTON HALL
Cheshire

This geometrical extravaganza is typical of the style of timber framing that appears in the houses of the gentry in the north-west. Diagonal braces are necessary to give a timber building rigidity, but here their function is more than simply structural: they have become a major decorative element. The pattern is emphasised by the blackening of the woodwork, contrasting with the whiteness of the plaster in between.

STOKESAY CASTLE
Craven Arms, Shropshire

The gatehouse at Stokesay was built of square timber panels, each of which has curved and diagonal braces that both strengthen and decorate it. The timber was left in its natural state; whether or not building timbers were blackened originally seems to have been very much a matter of local preference, and there is no doubt that much more woodwork is so treated now than ever was in the past. (However, unless it is clear that to blacken it has always been the local fashion, it is better to leave old timber bare, since oak lasts well without preservatives and black paint or tar are as likely to seal the wet in as to keep it out.) The projecting pegs may be the result of nineteenth-century repair, because originally these wooden pegs (sometimes called trenails because they hold the frame together) would have been cut off flush with the face of the timber.

More stage scenery than fortification, the Elizabethan gatehouse at Stokesay has a great deal of highly inventive carving. This lady is a sort of rustic Venus, a Renaissance nymph turned into a Shropshire lass. See also pp. 51, 65.

BECKLEY PARK
Oxfordshire

A favourite way of decorating brick buildings in the sixteenth century was to use burnt bricks to make zigzag patterns on the walls. The front of Beckley Park is covered with a network of diamonds formed of diagonal lines of black bricks. Such decoration can also be seen at Kirstead Hall, p. 77. See also p. 68.

EAST BARSHAM MANOR
Norfolk

The real explosion in brick building began in the late fifteenth century, when brick began to change from being a material used locally for want of anything better into a material which was sought after. East Barsham typifies many of the fashions of the age. Among other things, it contains fine examples of decorative brickwork like these terracotta portrait plaques. There may have been centres of production for work of this sort, in areas where suitable clay was to be found, but brickmakers travelled from one site to another and may have taken their moulds with them. Details of this kind appear on other buildings of the period in East Anglia and the south-east, where the lack of good stone encouraged the early development of brick. See also pp. 1, 27, 110, 111, 118.

NEW HALL

Elland, West Yorkshire

One thinks now of West Yorkshire as a region of stone houses, but many of the earliest houses in the area began as timber ones. Some, though partially rebuilt in stone, retain some of their older timber structure. At New Hall the front is entirely of stone (see p. 11), but at the back a considerable amount of its earlier framing is still visible. See also p. 125.

HALL I'TH'WOOD

Bolton, Greater Manchester

Hall I'Th'Wood is part-timber, part-stone, the stone part of the building having been built about seventy years later than the timber-framed wing which was originally self-contained, standing alone. There is absolutely no attempt to make the later, stone building conform in any way with the earlier work save in its convenience of planning. The idea that new work should respect and blend in with older building would have seemed very strange to people in the seventeenth century, when it was considered perfectly natural and proper for new building to be in an up-to-date style of architecture. See also pp. 35, 133.

GULLEGE

Nr East Grinstead, Sussex

Gullege has a stone front but is otherwise timber-framed. It is not certain whether the house was built like this or whether (as is perhaps more likely) the stone façade was added soon after 1600 in order to modernise the house and enhance the standing of its owner in much the same way that people in this century have sometimes clad the fronts of their houses with fake stonework. Stone was a prestige building material for the time and place, and the owner of Gullege sought to achieve the effect of a fashionable stone house without the expense of building one complete. See also p. 121.

THE RED HALL

Bourne, Lincolnshire

Bourne is on the edge of an area of good building stone, but also within an area where brick had been used for centuries before the building of the Red Hall in the 1620s. Indeed, it is a little surprising that the house is called Red Hall since there must have been a number of other distinctive red brick houses in the area by the time it was built. The fact that in this part of the country brick was not the novel material that it still was elsewhere may account for the use of stone for the most prominent part of the house, the porch and the front entrance. See also p. 33.

POUNDISFORD PARK

Pitminster, Somerset

The back of Poundisford is a wonderful pattern of golden stone, white walls and grey leadwork. The house is of stone, but only the windows, doors and quoins are of the fine, cut stone from Ham Hill. The rest of the walling is almost certainly quite rough rubble, concealed under a thick layer of lime-plaster render. The effect is to accentuate the contrast between walling and openings and to brighten the entire building. Many more such houses were originally rendered in this way than are now: too often the covering has since been removed, altering the building's appearance and leaving the stonework unprotected against the elements. (The worst treatment for this kind of wall, however, has been the application of modern cement, which is a recipe for disaster). See also p. 74.

BRADLEY MANOR

Newton Abbot, Devon

Lime render was popular in Devonshire for centuries, since it was an excellent way of keeping water out of the cob (earth) walls of ancient houses. The walls of Bradley Manor are actually of stone, but lime render was used in the same way, to brighten and weatherproof the rubble walls, and lime wash was even carried over the carved stonework of window surrounds. See also pp. 45, 138.

LEGH MANOR
Ansty, Sussex

Legh Manor is partly timber framed, but the timber is concealed and protected behind decorative tile-hanging. Such work was widespread in the south-east in the sixteenth and seventeenth centuries (its revival was immensely popular, too, with a number of late-Victorian architects from whom it was adopted in the twentieth century by hundreds of speculative builders all over the home counties).

WESTHOLME HALL
Winston, Durham

No less varied than walls are roofs. Like walls, roofs made use of whatever were the local resources – plain tiles or pantiles, thatch of various materials, and slates using a wide variety of different stones, requiring only that they could be split into sufficiently thin slabs. In some places such materials might be used in combination, as at Westholme Hall in County Durham, an early-seventeenth-century house, which has heavy stone slabs on the verges, where the rafters have their greatest strength, and tiles higher up to save weight. Gainford Hall, a few miles away, has an identical roof (page 32).

PHOTOGRAPHER'S NOTES AND ACKNOWLEDGMENTS

The secret of location photography is still the truism that one needs to be in the right place at the right time. Photographing buildings poses particular problems in this respect. As each house has a clearly defined topography, the sun moves around it in a particular way, dictating the ideal moment for photography. As far as possible I tried to ascertain in advance the direction in which the houses faced as there would be little point in trying to photograph an east-facing aspect in late afternoon on a sunny day. Another problem when photographing buildings at close range is that of distortion. A perspective control lens and a stepladder proved useful, but my preferred solution whenever possible was to shoot from a more distant viewpoint which, through the inclusion of the surroundings, gives a better sense of place.

I used both Leica and Hasselblad cameras with an extensive range of lenses. Films used were both Kodak and Fuji, with a predominance of Fuji 50 and 100 ASA. Filters were used sparingly to make fine adjustments in the colour balance.

My intention was to show the houses as they are today as a result of the many influences brought to bear on them by their past owners. It was good to see that many houses, which apparently twenty or thirty years ago were derelict, had been rescued to provide comfortable homes. By and large they had escaped over-restoration and had preserved the patina of centuries whilst bearing the imprint of their current owners. It is to many of these that I would like to extend my thanks for their warm welcome and assistance. Whilst it is impossible to name all who gave me generous help, I would like to thank the following in particular: Mrs Fielding, Mr and Mrs J. Sterck, Mr and Mrs G. Bartlett, Mr and Mrs M. Shellim, Captain J. H. and Mrs McBain, Mrs E. K. Lightburn, Mr and Mrs Ward-Thomas, Major and Mrs T. Binny, Baron G. de Dosza, Mr N. Helme, Lord Saye and Sele, Mr and Mrs Armitage, Mr and Mrs Woolner, Mr and Mrs Woodbridge, Mr and Mrs P. Gromett, Mr P. Herbert and Mr R. Rosewell.

I would also like to thank Diana Lanham and Mark Bainbridge of the National Trust and Mr Ulli Hintner of Leitz Instruments for their assistance. My thanks also to Robert and Nicolas Clark-Majerus for their enthusiastic support. Last but not least I would like to thank Colin Grant of Weidenfeld and Nicolson for the care he has taken over the production of this book.

INDEX

Numbers in italics refer to illustrations.